THE LOGIC OF THE HUMANITIES

Ernst Cassirer

THE LOGIC OF THE HUMANITIES

translated by
Clarence Smith Howe

New Haven and London: Yale University Press

Library of Congress catalog card number: 61–6311
ISBN: 0–300–00350–1 (cloth), 0–300–00035–9 (paper)

Distributed in Great Britain, Europe, and Africa by
Yale University Press, Ltd., London; in Canada by
McGill-Queen's University Press, Montreal; in Mexico
by Centro Interamericano de Libros Académicos,
Mexico City; in Central and South America by Kaiman
& Polon, Inc., New York City; in Australasia by
Australia and New Zealand Book Co., Pty., Ltd.,
Artarmon, New South Wales; in India by UBS Publishers'
Distributors Pvt., Ltd., Delhi; in Japan by John
Weatherhill, Inc., Tokyo.

CONTENTS

Translator's Foreword

WE LIVE IN an age in which the efforts of the individual appear to count for very little, in which it is all too easy to assume that events will "have their way" regardless of how we vote, act, or think. More serious still, we are very easily persuaded to the abject conclusion that even how we individually vote, act, and think is actually nothing more than the complex result of subtle forces working upon us from countless hidden corners of our physical being and our culture. As for the truly great advances and achievements in our cultural life, we are all too ready to assume that they have resulted from the irrepressible unfolding of natural genius.

It is not surprising, then, that the centennial celebration of the publication of Darwin's *Origin of Species* has occasioned revivals, in modern dress, of that fashionable nineteenth-century hope that "natural science will be able to demonstrate a certain and on-going evolution in man's physical make-up and in his cultural achievements," frequently with the implication that there is some necessary connection between a predominance of individuals with I.Q.'s over 180 and an age of great cultural efflorescence. In short, we are still prone to put our "faith in the coming of a better world" in the lap of natural science, especially a projected science of eugenics. I do not wish to argue that there is no connec-

tion whatever between selectively improving the human
frame and raising our cultural attainments. As Plato has
said, it is a "useful myth"; it buoys our hopes and stirs our
imaginations, just so long as it cannot be shown to be completely groundless.

In contrast to this empirically oriented picture of man,
Ernst Cassirer's philosophy of culture is sobering indeed.
But, on second thought, many of us will find it a more
meaningful and a more challenging cultural "myth." Those
readers familiar with Cassirer's *Essay on Man* and his extensive study of concept formation in the various sciences
cannot help feeling added regret that he did not live long
enough to take part in the Darwin-centennial discussions of
man's physical and cultural "evolution." Fortunately, in
The Logic of the Humanities we have Cassirer's most detailed and mature treatment of this subject. Moreover,
approximately two years before writing this work, he had
written a brief historical and analytical essay on determin-
istic and humanistic attempts, since the Renaissance, to
formulate the pattern of man's cultural "evolution." That
essay appeared as "Naturalistische und humanistische Begründung der Kulturphilosophie" and is included here as
an appropriate introduction to his own more extensive and
systematic *Logic of the Humanities.*

The non-German reader of this work deserves a few
helpful suggestions of a linguistic nature. In particular, the
two words *Geist* and *Wissenschaft,* in their various phras-
ings, have caused the translator hours of word searching,
and not always with the happiest of results. It is hardly too
much to say that a valuable and comprehensive intellectual
history of Germany could result from a history-of-ideas
study of what makes these two words peculiarly German.
The chief philosophic difficulty which they present to any-

one attempting an English translation is that their possible meanings are more various and, at the same time, more unified than are those of their English equivalents. So far as I know, in English we have no working concept comprehensive, at once, of all conscious and unconscious "self-awareness"; and "self-awareness" is, of course, a lame expression for what I have reference to; for what I have in mind is *awareness of* one's "thinking self" *being in direct confrontation with* the object of an act of awareness. Thus most dream experience and our self-involved yearnings would also be included in this "life of the mind." Couple to such "self-awareness," of being in direct confrontation with objects, awareness of "personal otherness" and one is close to the all-inclusive domain of reference for which *Geist* is the German name. But it comprehends, also, all the achievements of mind in this subjective sense, which, as contributions to the shape of the physical world, are non-personal—what Hegel called "objective mind."

Similarly with *Wissenschaft,* the English reader is uneasy and usually indignant at the suggestion that there are "sciences" other than the exact natural sciences. Thus, to borrow a now popular piece of philosophical jargon, one could, in German thought, subtitle Cassirer's *Logic of the Humanities* a "meta-science of the science of culture"; for what I have usually translated as "humanities" translates more literally as "cultural sciences," and the word *Logik* stands for a conceptual framework by use of which the various "cultural sciences" can themselves be better understood. Thus, any rigorously systematic conceptual framework—that of mathematics, jurisprudence, theology, etc.— is easily referred to, in German, as a science.

Whereas the German philosopher spends a sizable proportion of his time trying to find a satisfactory scheme by

which to sort out from each other important aspects of
Geist (mind) and branches of *Wissenschaft* (science), his
English speaking counterpart is more likely here to busy
himself with pioneer border concepts and novel inter-dis-
ciplinary studies.

It may be helpful, also, to make a few suggestions as to
the place of Cassirer's *Logic of the Humanities* within his
philosophical position as a whole. Cassirer's lasting contributions to the history of philosophy are beyond question;
his original contributions to philosophy are far more difficult to assess. Here he was not a system builder but a path-
finder to new directions. However, I am convinced that a
careful study of the following work will reveal that Cassirer
has achieved nothing short of a genuine *tour de force* in
treating the metaphysical problem as to "mind and its place
in nature." Though he has deliberately shunned giving it
systematic, metaphysical formulation, he has succeeded in
working out a perfectly consistent "idealistic naturalism,"
if we may call it that.

In the *Logic*, and elsewhere, Cassirer is a severe critic of
French naturalism. Nevertheless, his own treatment of
mental phenomena is as naturalistic as John Dewey's in
most of its features, as the following work will show, though
his language is still comfortably idealistic and his method
of showing the relation of meanings to natural processes
is significantly different.

This rapprochement between idealism and naturalism is
not limited to Cassirer and Dewey. Indeed it characterizes
one of the most significant tendencies in modern philosophy since the decline of Hegelian absolutism in the latter
half of the nineteenth century. In this period of disillusionment a growing number of idealists, men like Emile Bou-
troux in France and Herman Cohen in Germany, were

determined to avoid a return to the Kantian dualism between mind and matter while salvaging, at the same time, the legitimate claims of idealism from the shipwreck of its Hegelian pomposities. Meanwhile, among those more at home with the philosophical concepts of naturalism, we detect an equally serious determination to avoid crude and facile attempts at reducing the world of the mind to *nothing but* the working of natural processes, in short, to do justice to the claims of idealism. Here one thinks especially of F.J.E. Woodbridge and George H. Mead and, to a lesser extent, of Charles Peirce and William James. But this effort toward finding the proper place of mind in nature is most clearly seen within the persistent shift in John Dewey's thinking on this issue.

From an early behavioristic analysis of mind as experience, Dewey moves more and more toward the conviction that "experience" is too subjective a word to stand for the dominant features of mental phenomena. It is highly significant that, late in his life, he realized that "culture" is a far more accurate word for the objective and cooperative features of mind in its natural setting than was the earlier word "experience." In coming to this realization Dewey has arrived at the same basic conviction that underlies Cassirer's Philosophy of Symbolic Forms—that culture in its manifold forms *is* "mind's place in nature."

Cassirer's insight on this issue was remarkably clear very early in his career. The highly subjective concept of mind found in the popular Empiro-Criticism of Richard Avenarius had had a strong influence not only upon Ernst Mach's Phenomenalism but also upon the shaping of William James' Radical Empiricism. It is just this radical subjectivism in the philosophy of William James which Cassirer found occasion to criticize in his *Substance and Function*

(1910), while praising the "objective relativism" of Mead
and Dewey in his reference to the Chicago School. British
philosophy has shown little inclination, except for a few
neo-Hegelians like Bradley, to identify mind and culture;
accordingly, it is still busily concerned with the unbridge-
able gulf between mind and nature. Fresh as his thinking
in philosophy was, Alfred North Whitehead still found
himself wrestling mightily with this problem. The strain of
pragmatism in his attempts to relate mind and natural
processes is still grounded in the pure-and-immediate-ex-
perience concepts of James, rather than in the social and
cultural contextualism of Mead and Dewey.

Accordingly, Cassirer begins his systematic treatment of
the logic of the humanities with a demonstration of the im-
possibility of ever bridging that "gulf between minds" implied by James' radical empiricist account of "mind" and
"self." But Cassirer's alternative thesis, that living culture
is the cooperation of one mind with another and, as such,
the locus of mind in nature, is not presented as a formal
metaphysical argument. It is "a philosophy of idealistic
naturalism" only by implication. In his reluctance to translate his *functional* analysis of "mind, self, and culture" into
metaphysical jargon, he reminds us, once again, of John
Dewey and, even more, of George H. Mead.

But as soon as we ask what Cassirer means by culture, interesting differences begin to emerge between his account
of "mind, self, and society" and that of the Chicago School.
To appreciate this difference, it is helpful to refer, again,
to the two German words mentioned above, *Geist* and *Wissenschaft*. Cassirer has arrived at his cultural interpretation
of mind and self under the influence of the attempts by
Dilthey and his followers to give philosophical grounding
to the so-called *Geisteswissenschaften,* which we awkwardly

translate as "the social sciences." In his last writings Dilthey had already come to the conclusion that it would be far better to name these sciences of human nature *Kulturwissenschaften;* it is a shift paralleled in many respects by Dewey's somewhat later decision to move from his interpretation of mind as "experience" to its analysis as "culture."

This is not to say that Dilthey and his followers have fully anticipated Cassirer's analysis of mind and self as cultural phenomena. For they have done little more than divide their study of human nature into "personal experience" and study of the historical relativism of our more exact sciences of man—what Max Scheler later came to call "the sociology of knowledge"—continuing, in effect, to regard mind in the traditional concepts of subjective idealism while thinking of culture as its historically conditioned expression. To Cassirer, the utterly subjective aspect of mind and self called "personal experience" is, in the final analysis, either mere natural process or mere sensation. For him, *all cognitive* aspects of mind, all aspects concerned with meaning (rather than with those direct experiences which mediate meanings) are *social;* and, if given lasting communicable form, they are *cultural.*

But the *Kulturwissenschaften,* for which Cassirer and his predecessors are seeking the basic logic, are not to be facilely identified with what the English-speaking world refers to as "the social sciences." For we are far too inclined to think of these as exact natural sciences for the identification to be accurate. The Germans, and especially Cassirer, are inclined to classify the American and English social sciences as *Naturwissenschaften,* exact sciences of empirical human *nature.* As suggested above, the German concept of science *(Wissenschaft)* is far broader than its

English counterpart, in that it includes any systematic ordering of concepts, such as in mathematics, jurisprudence, or theology. In this wider meaning, "science" is not concerned with factual descriptions and the exact lawful relationships obtaining between natural events. Rather, it is science in the ancient sense of being a profounder or more adequate *knowledge of* what we already "know" in the factual sense of our direct and daily encounter of the world and ourselves. Thus, even poetry and mythology can be the concern of that disciplined knowledge which is *Kulturwissenschaft*. It is precisely for this reason that I have chosen to translate *Kulturwissenschaften* as "the humanities."

Hence, Cassirer's *Logic of the Humanities* is an analysis of those basic concepts which underlie our arts, our knowledge of history, and our disciplined knowledge of human nature. The value of a study of these concepts and their interrelationships is that it enables us to see more in a work of art, or in our direct encounter with human personality, than we otherwise would. It is *the study of disciplined perception*, whether of the eye or the ear; as such, it is *a logic of concrete universals*. This concreteness, directness, and wholeness are precisely what distinguish the logic of the humanities from the traditional logic of abstract universals. Initially, the universals in either logic are all those vaguely concrete concepts of our everyday thought. But, as the logic of the humanities advances, these universals acquire ever richer, subtler, and more concrete wholeness; whereas the logic of the natural sciences works continually toward *isolation of generalized aspects*, abstractions which hold uniformly and equally for all individuals or events in a given domain. And whereas the former involves the cognitive processes ever more intimately in perceptual experience, the latter frees the mind from such "total" involvement in perception. The difference is primarily that of orientation in thought and of the appropriate development of techniques and concepts for furthering the advance of these divergent orientations. Thus one of Cassirer's central concerns in *The Logic of the Humanities* is to disentangle the analytical study of personality, as such, from the work of those exact sciences engaged in discovering the mathematically formulable processes of nature in which personality necessarily finds its embodiment and expression. As such, it is neither a study of what is utterly unique in particular personalities nor a study of the so-called "stream of history." Instead, it is a logic of style concepts, upon which we consciously, or unconsciously, build up our understanding of particular persons and of historical events.

In contrast to an exact science of the laws of nature, such a logic of styles is "reliable" knowledge, not because it enables us to predict personal behavior or historical events, but because it brings us to a deeper knowledge of what we already know about human nature (in terms both of unreflected daily experience and of scientific knowledge in that exact empirical sense). The concepts of this "logic" teach us to see more subtly and more profoundly, not the *how,* but the *what* of "human nature." The term "logic," then, is here to be taken as referring simply to a critical study of such type and style concepts and not to a supposed methodology of historical predictions or of formulas for artistic creation.

It should also be noted that the word "humanities" in English commonly includes the practice of the creative arts. As a translation of Cassirer's term *Kulturwissenschaften,* it never implies such a direct reference to the arts. However, exactly as in the case of history, the arts are indirectly under discussion, both as data for critical study, and to the extent

that they necessitate in their creation a recognition of concepts of style in perceptual form, even if only unconsciously. Indeed, Cassirer is thinking more directly of analysis of
our creative achievements in art, myth, language, and religion, than of analysis of particular historical personalities
when he speaks of this logic as a "logic of self-knowledge."
Hence, for him, "true" history is not only a knowledge of
particulars; it is also a "poetic knowledge" of human possibilities and, as such, it derives its intelligibility through the
functioning, critically or unconsciously, of the "logic" of
style concepts.

Cassirer's conception of the humanistic disciplines as
"sciences" in their own right stems from a German intellectual tradition at least as old as Lessing. Thus, for Lessing,
Herder, Schiller, Goethe, Wilhelm von Humboldt, Hegel,
and many others, *Kultur* has its ancient humanistic meaning of a cultivation or "education of the human race." In
his "Naturalistische und humanistische Begründung der
Kulturphilosophie," Cassirer has brilliantly demonstrated
that this new German humanism was more than simply a revival of that ancient Stoic conception of education as the
cultivation and nurture of the merely natural human plant,
that, in addition, it conceived of human nature as the po-
tentiality for *self-definition,* as the only product of nature
capable, not only of learning from a teacher, but of *teaching
itself.* This historical sketch alone makes the essay an indispensable Introduction to the *Logic.* Cassirer might also
have added that it was a man who regarded himself as a
neo-Stoic, the third Earl of Shaftesbury, who had supplied
the guiding vision for this new German humanism and
that, as such, he was probably echoing, as part of the Platonic Renaissance in England, Pico della Mirandola's *Ora-
tion on the Dignity of Man.*

Cassirer's German predecessors, following Leibniz, have taken this humanistic concept out of its ancient rhetorical context and, with few exceptions, have sought to give it unity and "scientific" rigor by welding it to theories of historical evolution. In the following work Cassirer is endeavoring to give the humanistic disciplines "scientific" rigor while freeing them from such historical connections and dogmas.

Elsewhere, I have sought to show that the chief contribution to philosophy of Cassirer's analysis of the humanistic disciplines is that, admitting the ubiquity of natural process in all experience, he goes on to demonstrate that questions of logic, of definition, are necessarily prior to any intelligent, scientifically soluble, questions as to the emergence of such thoughts *as products of nature,* thus making obvious the all-too-common tendency of naturalistic philosophies to embrace uncritically this or that theory purporting to prove that meaning and form are identical with the natural processes, or cooperations of processes, which maintain them and bring them into being; for, as such, they are no more the thinking process than "what is seen" is the seeing process; they are *merely* the logical or formal aspect of such supporting and encompassing existential situations. At the same time, Cassirer avoids the opposite tendency, that of defining man's consciousness of himself as identical with an "existential" situation beyond the reach of natural process. It is because of this treatment of thought and object of thought that I look upon Cassirer's philosophical position as a fresh and perfectly consistent "idealistic naturalism." Elsewhere, I have sought to show the importance of avoiding these alternative pitfalls with respect to the distinction between the logical and the existential by an extensive comparison of Cassirer's thought to that of Dewey, in the one regard, and to that of Heidegger, in the other. Although, in my opinion, Cassirer's philosophic position is far closer to Dewey's than to Heidegger's, it must not be thought that there are no important differences between Cassirer and Dewey. For Dewey's ultimate interest, like that of Hegel, is to locate the rational in the actual; Cassirer's ultimate concern, like that of Kant, is to make certain that our categories of analysis are never reduced to *nothing but* states of affairs.

C. S. H.

Humboldt State College
September 1960

Acknowledgments

THIS TRANSLATION was begun as partial fulfillment of the requirements for the doctoral degree in philosophy at Columbia University. In this connection, I owe particular thanks to Professor James Gutmann who served as sponsor of my dissertation work. His devotion to my proposal to translate Cassirer's *Logik der Kulturwissenschaften* was like that of a father for the success of his son. I owe thanks also to his wife, who, with her husband, spent hours carefully checking the translation. I shall always be grateful to Professor John Herman Randall, Jr., for his immediate understanding and encouragement of my interest in Ernst Cassirer's contributions to philosophy. For what little I may know of the history of philosophy, I owe more to him than to any other living person. To Professor Paul O. Kristeller I owe a deeper knowledge of the German intellectual tradition in which Cassirer's thought developed. I am grateful to Professor Horace Friess for his scholarly generosity and kind words of encouragement. To Professors Danto, Hieatt, and Sokel, also of Columbia University, I owe many helpful suggestions. I should like, belatedly, to express my long-felt indebtedness to Professor Arnold Bergstraesser, formerly of the University of Chicago, for giving me my first and unforgettable glimpse of the humanistic tradition in Germany. My thanks, also, to Professor John E. Smith of

Yale for first bringing this translation to the attention of Yale University Press. I am especially grateful for the wise counsel and keen interest of Professor Charles Hendel. The publication of this translation owes much to him. My deepest thanks, also, to Benjamin F. Houston, editor of Yale University Press. I am most grateful to Mrs. Cassirer, without whose interest and kind permission this publication would not have been possible. My conversations with her were among the highlights of my days at Columbia. Finally, I owe my greatest debt to my wife Marjorie. I could not have taken on this project without her complete devotion and expert secretarial skills. Her help to me has been so constant and so manifold that I find it meaningless to distinguish my own contributions from hers.

C. S. H.

INTRODUCTION

INTRODUCTION

Naturalistic and Humanistic Philosophies of Culture

PHILOSOPHY OF CULTURE is surely the most questionable and the most disputed of all the various branches which we now distinguish within the systematic whole of philosophy. At present, the very concept is far from being sharply defined, nor is its meaning generally agreed upon. What we are faced with here is not only a lack of firm and recognized solutions to this fundamental problem of definition; there is an even more elementary lack of understanding as to what *questions* are meaningful or relevant to the study of culture. This extraordinary uncertainty stems in part from the fact that the philosophic study of culture is the youngest among the disciplines of philosophy; for, unlike the others, it cannot look back upon a secure tradition of development through the centuries. The division of philosophy into three main fields—logic, physics, and ethics—was already complete in antiquity and it has continued to be firmly maintained ever since, virtually unaltered. Kant still recognized this threefold division as valid, declaring that it conforms perfectly to the nature of things and permits of no improvement.[1]

1. Kant, "Grundlegung zur Metaphysik der Zitten," *Werke* (Berlin: Bruno Cassirer, 1912–1918), IV, 243.

Only gradually did modern thinkers realize that, in addition to logic, moral philosophy, and physics, there are other distinct modes and directions for philosophic inquiry. To be sure, in this regard the period of the Renaissance marks the opening beat to a definite and original evolution in philosophic awareness. Throughout the sixteenth and seventeenth centuries we detect the ripening of a new philosophic problem; it is the working out of what Dilthey has called "the natural system of the cultural sciences." But this "natural system of the cultural sciences," which concealed within itself the first bud of a future philosophy of culture, continued to remain lost within the established philosophic systems, as if homeless. What was new here and just beginning to stir itself was retarded and repressed.

However, this restriction was no merely peripheral or accidental circumstance. It originated in the most robustly positive and productive force holding sway over those first centuries of the modern mind. For it was mathematics and mathematical natural science which fashioned the ideal of knowledge of this age; and, aside from geometry, analysis, and mechanics, there appeared to be no room for any other truly rigorous scientific inquiry. Accordingly, if the cultural world were ever to be made accessible and self-evident to philosophic reason, if it were not to remain in mystical darkness, in the chains of theological tradition, it, too, must be clear and mathematically formulable, precisely as the physical cosmos. On the strength of this guiding vision, Spinoza attempted to supply the missing systematic unity between ethics and geometry. No longer is the human world to remain a "state within the state." From now on, we are to observe and describe man and his work as if these were but lines, planes, and bodies. The Spinozistic doctrine of unity, which is a rigorously methodological, as well as metaphysical monism, ultimately demands this treatment of ethical questions. Accordingly, with adequate philosophical knowledge, the notion of purpose is, of necessity, denied and extinguished; for, if we trace out its origin, it becomes clear that it is nothing but an anthropomorphic error and falsification, whereas truth is reached exclusively by purely mathematical and lawful concepts.

Subsequent thought was profoundly influenced by Spinoza's methodological monism. And in the reawakening of Spinozistic thought which took place toward the end of the eighteenth century, this very demand for unity constitutes an important and decisive motif. It was here that Schelling was able to tie his thought directly to that of Spinoza. He openly declared that his philosophy of identity sought to be nothing other than the completion of what Spinoza had set forth in an initial and bold sketch. In Schelling's "Presentation of My System of Philosophy," in the year 1801, we find the following statement:

> It is the nature of philosophy to observe things as they are in themselves, that is to say, insofar as they are the infinite and absolute identity itself. Thus, true philosophy consists in the proof that the absolute Identity (the Infinite) cannot alienate itself, and that all that is, insofar as it is, is necessarily the Infinite itself—an argument which, of all previous philosophers, only Spinoza has recognized, although he has not given the complete proof for it, nor has he expressed it with sufficient clarity to prevent its being almost universally misunderstood.[2]

2. Friedrich von Schelling, "Darstellung meines System der Philosophie," *Sämmtliche Werke* (Stuttgart and Augsburg: J. G. Cotta, 1856–61), IV, 120.

But, in spite of Schelling's assurance as to agreement and complete unanimity between his doctrine and that of Spinoza, it is not possible for him to take up the problem precisely as Spinoza had left it. True, he also contends for an absolute identity between mind and nature; still, for him, one of the members of this equation—the concept of nature—has undergone a fundamental transformation. When Schelling speaks of nature, he is not thinking of a being that creates itself mechanically through extension and motion. Nature, for him, is not simply a sum total of geometric arrangements and mechanical laws, but an organic whole of structures and powers. For him, mathematical physics sinks to a mere abstraction, to a shadow. Nature possesses true reality only in the form of organic events and organic structures. Philosophical thought lifts itself from this first stage of being to the true world of Spirit, to the world of history and culture. From theoretical philosophy, which teaches us the laws of space and time, matter and force, the path of philosophy leads past the world of practical consciousness to the highest stage—to the stage of aesthetic intuition. "Nature is a poem, wrapped in secret and wondrous form. Could the riddle but reveal itself, it would show us that marvelously deceptive odyssey of Spirit, which in seeking itself flees itself; for through the world of sense, as through the words of sense, it gazes upon that land of phantasy which we yearn for through translucent mist."[3]

The philosophy of culture which came to expression in Romanticism developed from this guiding vision in Schelling's system. Its strength and its weakness lie in the fact that it seeks to illuminate by a single principle and comprehend within a single view all manifestations of conscious-

3. Schelling, "System des transzendentalen Idealismus," *Sämmtliche Werke*, II, 628.

ness: the first dreamy dawning of myth; folk legend and poetry; and, finally, the highest manifestations of thought, the maturest expressions of language, science, and philosophy. The "land of phantasy," of which Schelling speaks, and the field of strictly logical knowledge are constantly influencing each other. Instead of being distinct domains of knowledge, they involve each other. Romanticism created its highest achievements from this power of imagination and intuition. It not only saw nature in a new perspective; in and by virtue of this insight, it succeeded in gaining one synoptic grasp of all forms of spiritual reality. Here for the first time the deep and authentic sources of myth and religion, language and poetry, morals and law appeared to have been brought to light. Such names alone as Eichhorn and Savigny, Jakob Grimm, and August Boeckh serve to indicate what this movement performed and signified with respect to the establishment of the history of law and language, and our knowledge of classical antiquity. It cannot be doubted that Romantic philosophy had prepared the way for this enormous scientific work, and it has inspired it in particular ways again and again.

Yet there was one principle for which this philosophy could not, and did not dare, inquire in any strictly logical sense. It had already denied itself this question; for, to raise it would be to bring back into the light of investigation what the fundamental conviction of Romanticism had declared to be forever inscrutable, inaccessible to the understanding. If it were to seek a *principle* here, it could not be a logical principle, but only the statement of a half-mystical *beginning*. For Romanticism, this source of all things spiritual, which is at once manifest and hidden, has its being in the "Spirit of the people" [*"Volksgeist"*].

This, too, is a naturalism, although it speaks the language of a spiritualistic metaphysics. For here history and culture have been taken back into the womb of organic life. They possess no genuine "autonomy," no independence or *inner lawfulness*. Here they no longer take their rise from an original spontaneity of the self; they are a tranquil process [*Werden*] and growth, which merely becomes, as it were; like the seed which only needs to be planted in the earth in order to become a tree, so law, language, art, and morality have grown from the original power of the national spirit. This tranquillity and complete certainty implies a quietistic principle. The world of culture is no longer seen as a world of free act; it is lived as a fate. In this sense, for example, Savigny has sought to ground all development of law in custom, habit, and popular belief and to limit it to these spheres, continually emphasizing that true law can only develop through such "silent inner forces." Thus Theodor Litt, in his *Individuum und Gemeinschaft,* a particularly clear and penetrating methodological critique of the ideas basic to these organic systems of metaphysics, makes the following remark:

> The excellence and charm of a philosophy of organism consists in the fact that it presents with self-evident craftsmanship, and in the dreamlike certainty of plant existence, the imperturbable working of a force, for which all convulsions and inner strife in the course of the world's development signify only a ripple on the surface; its weakness is that it . . . allows the dissolution of personal existence, an irremovable feature of this doctrine, to become so obvious.[4]

4. Theodor Litt, *Individuum und Gemeinschaft; Grundlegung der Kulturphilosophie,* 2nd ed. (Leipzig and Berlin: B. G. Teubner, 1924), p. 153.

To be sure, this weakness and danger first became fully evident when the veil in which Romanticism had enveloped nature and history tore into shreds. This happened when the desire to know was no longer content with losing itself in sheer perceptual awe of the wellsprings of life, but demanded instead a *knowledge* of life. At this juncture, Schelling's philosophy of nature was abandoned; the ideal of a purely empirical science, which was to explain both biological and "psychic" phenomena, took its place. This universal science of life (theoretical biology) was also destined to become the prototype and standard for all historical observations and all philosophy of culture.

This turn of events consummated itself in the second half of the nineteenth century and found its clearest expression in French cultural philosophy. The thinkers who belong to this circle acquired their philosophical schooling from Comte's *Cours de Philosophie positive;* this basic text of positivism determined their method and their problems. But the state of science at this time had an even stronger influence on them than did these general philosophical presuppositions. The concept of the universe which they met with here, and which they regarded as definitive, was that of classical physics. The highest axiom of this physics was the principle of causality, as construed in the famous hypothesis of the "Laplacean mind."

Even critically minded thinkers schooled in Kant did not dare to undermine this interpretation. A particularly concise and solid piece of writing by Otto Liebmann stands out in this regard. In his *Die Klimax der Theorien* Liebmann begins by showing that the assumption of complete determinism would also apply to all fields of human thought, to all modes of research, and to all knowledge, and that in this respect not the least difference obtains between the sciences of the moral world and those of the physical world.

Whether it is a question of the motions of stars and atoms or of market prices and exchange rates; whether the succession of geological revolutions and metamorphoses of our earth or the folklore lost with Livy's early history of Rome are to be reconstructed; whether characters, decisions, and actions or ocean-currents and meteorological processes are in question: in every possible instance, rational science, as distinguished from childish superstition, depends upon the universal assumption that a strict causal nexus underlies even our consideration of inaccessible reaches of overt events, and that such partial events exactly match the otherwise sporadic and fragmented pattern of our experience of this causal nexus. Still, the difficult problem— that of reconciling this fundamental scientific conviction with moral freedom of the will and with logical freedom of thought—is transcendent; but regardless of how the solution is sought, it absolutely must not be allowed to interfere with the epistemological questions. This would be an extraneous and disruptive intrusion and would only create confusion. The problem of freedom has no place here. *"Disbelief* in miracles" is conceptually equivalent to, or synonymous with, *"believing* firmly in the absolute lawfulness of all events, without exception." It is *to have absolutely no doubt* as to the unconditioned, objective, and universal validity of the causal principle: these two are simply equivalent concepts or synonyms.[5]

5. Liebmann, *Die Klimax der Theorien, Eine Untersuchung aus dem Bereich allgemeinen Wissenschaftslehre* (Strassburg, 1884), pp. 87 ff.

I have adduced these statements because they characterize in an extraordinarily concise and penetrating manner the underlying, problematic state of affairs common to natural science and philosophy in the second half of the nineteenth century. Both fields of inquiry see themselves faced with a decision which they seem unable to avoid. They must either accept the ideal of the "Laplacean mind" or admit to belief in miracles. Under these circumstances, there could be no doubt for the epistemologist and the critical philosopher as to how the scales were tipped.

Today, of course, as we read these sentences of Liebmann, a peculiar feeling comes over us. They were written only some fifty years ago; but epistemology and the philosophy of science have undergone an almost total change in this brief space of time. Today, no student of epistemology would dare to introduce the principle of universal determinism in the form which Liebmann gave to it. For he would immediately find himself faced with all the serious questioning and doubt on this score to which the development of modern theoretical physics has led. I do not believe that this doubt entails any real threat to the principle of causality, as such, or that it forces us to an absolute avowal of indeterminism. However, it does demand that we reexamine what is, and what is not, implied in the universal principle of causality. But I do not intend to go into this problem in this connection for I have given an exhaustive analysis of it elsewhere.[6] Instead of this, my concern here is merely to focus attention on the consequences which the principle of universal determinism has had upon the sub-

6. See my *Determinism and Indeterminism in Modern Physics, Historical and Systematic Studies of the Problem of Causality* (New Haven: Yale University Press, 1956).

sequent growth of the humanities and upon the attempts
to establish a philosophy of culture.

The French philosophers of culture were the first to address themselves to this problem; and, although they make
a show of taking exact physics as their model, they were
neither mathematicians nor physicists. Their interest moves
in another direction. Their fundamental orientation is
determined, not according to the world view of Newton or
Laplace, but according to that of Darwin and Spencer.
Here too, as with Schelling and just as in the nature philosophy of Romanticism, nature and culture are joined and
reduced, as it were, to a common denominator, with the
result that both were subject to a common law, the fundamental law of evolution. But the reduction in this equation has changed; its value is now, so to speak, in the opposite medium of exchange. For the difference which appears
to obtain between nature and culture is no longer to be
bridged, as in Romanticism, through a spiritualization of
nature, but through a materialization of culture. Thus, if
a genuine science of culture is to be achieved, it is not metaphysics or theology which must lead the way, but chemistry
and physics, zoology and botany, anatomy and physiology.
Intuitively, organism is still adhered to but, in the final
analysis, it necessarily reduces to mechanism and totally
loses itself in it.

One of the first of this school of thought, who not only
championed it but engaged in it with genuine talent, was
Sainte-Beuve. He was not a philosopher, nor could one by
any means describe him as a systematic or exact scientist
of any particular field. His genuine talents lay not with
generalities or basic principles but in his manifold knowledge of particulars, in perceptual knowledge of the subtlest
details. In this respect, he opened up wholly new treasures

for the study of cultural history. His influence on French circles of thought was so great that Anatole France has referred to him as the *doctor universalis* of the nineteenth century. He preferred to characterize his own work as natural research in the *domain* of the mind; he sought to be "a naturalist of the human psyche."[7]

What Sainte-Beuve practiced with effortless virtuosity and matchless feel was first developed into a fixed and thoroughgoing method by his famous disciple Hyppolyte Taine. It was Taine who first introduced a fixed causal schema which claimed to be valid for all future analysis of cultural history. He devised that triad which, according to him, encompasses all explanation of individual phenomena —the triad of race, place, and time. Once we have a correct and firm grasp of these three fundamental factors, we have a complete understanding of any problem of intellectual history. In correctly combining these factors we are also able, as it were, to conjure from them the entire sweep of historical events and of cultural phenomena in all their iridescent splendor. And one cannot deny that in his masterpieces, in *Histoire de la Littérature Anglaise* and in *Philosophie de l'Art,* Taine has succeeded in working this piece of magic. He never tires of drawing together countless numbers of particular instances for the purpose of shedding light on the character and intellectual climate of a given age. However, in gathering his data he follows no specific or methodical plan. He collects it whenever he is lucky enough to find it; and, wherever he finds it, he accepts it uncritically. An anecdote is fully as valuable to him as an historical record or other documentary evidence. A remark in a sermon, a contemporary satire, or a memoir, is acknowledged

7. In this regard see Irving Babbitt, *The Masters of Modern French Criticism* (Boston and New York: Houghton Mifflin and Co., 1912).

without much scruple and fitted in where needed. It is from such individual but characteristic touches, which Taine himself calls *de tout petits faits significatifs,* that he builds up his portraits.

But Taine is well aware that a mere putting together of particular facts can never lead to a firmly grounded scientific *theory.* According to him, the last part of the establishment of a theory is its constructive and deductive part. *Après la collection des faits la recherche des causes,* after the selection of empirical data, there comes the search for the causes from which these data result. According to Taine, it is not hard to discover these causes, so long as we remain true to the first principles of positivism. These are to be seen as purely *immanent,* rather than *transcendent* causes. Unlike the suprapersonal unities and wholes of Romantic philosophies, they do not belong to a supersensible world; they are the same forces which shape and dominate the material world. As Taine puts it in the introduction to his *Philosophie de l'Art,*

> The modern method which I endeavor to follow, and which has now begun to penetrate all the sciences, consists in viewing all human creations, and works of art in particular, as facts and products whose distinguishing features are to be laid bare and whose causes are to be traced, nothing more. Thus, science neither judges nor justifies; its task is merely to establish and to explain. Cultural science must employ the same methods as botany, which studies the orange tree and the pear, the spruce and the birch as of equal importance. Indeed, cultural science is nothing other than a form of applied botany, concerned not with plants but with human achievements. Thus it belongs to that

universal movement in which, today, the humanities *(sciences morales)* and the natural sciences are approaching each other and in which the former are beginning to achieve the same certainty and progress that characterize the latter.

Thus, categorizing one group of facts as physical and another as intellectual or moral may perhaps point to an inherent difference; but, as regards the manner of our *knowledge* of them, this circumstance is completely irrelevant. For in neither case are we concerned with knowledge of particular facts as such, but only with their causal nexus, and in both instances this is of the same nature and the same stringency.

There are causes for ambition, courage, or truthfulness in precisely the same sense as for digestion, muscular movement, or animal heat. Vice and virtue are products just as sulphuric acid and sugar are; each complex being comes to be out of the union of other more elemental substances, without which it could not exist. Thus, we ferret out the constitutive facts of moral character precisely as we seek to analyze psychological make-up. There is one chain of all-powerful and universal causes whose work is the universal structure of things and the overriding shape of events. Religions, philosophy, poetry, industry, and technology, the forms of society and family are nothing other than the stamp which events have taken on through the working of these universal causes.

Thus Taine is able to announce with pride that, "Today, history, like zoology, has found its science of anatomy;

moreover, we know to which branch of this science we must turn in order to be able to answer a philological, linguistic, or mythological question. Always, we are obliged to proceed in this [architechtonic] fashion if we are to continue to arrive at new and fruitful results."[8]

Theories of universal determinism can proceed in three different directions and with three systematically different basic assumptions. These basic assumptions can be differentiated as physical, psychological, and metaphysical. The first of these has received its clearest formulation in the work of the French Positivists—Comte, Sainte-Beuve, Renan, and Taine. The second is exemplified, in contemporary philosophy, in Spengler's philosophy of culture. Hegel's Philosophy of History and Phenomenology of Mind are representative of the third.

The physicalistic proof of strict determinism begins with the assumption that all events in the human world are subject to the laws of nature and that they are the outgrowth of *fixed* natural conditions. The physical state of affairs, the nature of the land, the climate, the laws of heredity and of societal heritage: these are the basal factors underlying all events and through which they are completely and unequivocally determined. There is no spontaneity of the ego enabling it to break through these laws to refashion these factors. To be sure, even in this theory the activity of the ego does not allow itself to be completely suppressed. For this activity plays some part, however modest, in the theory of evolution, which contains the framework for it, acknowledging and anticipating it. The theory implies that the individual being is not rigidly dovetailed to its environment and, hence, lost in this dovetailing, but that it

8. Taine, *Histoire de la Littérature Anglaise,* Introduction, 8th ed. (Paris: Librairie Hachette, 1892), pp. ix ff.

"adjusts" to it and, therefore, can modify itself within fixed limits. In order to give expression to both of these aspects of the concept of evolution, Comte has coined the curious notion of a "modifiable fate," a *"fatalité modifiable"*—a concept meant to be taken as empirical and positive but of which it must, of course, be said that in precariousness and antinomic disagreement it probably has no equal among Comte's beleaguered metaphysical concepts.[9]

The second form of historical fatalism, which I have termed psychological, is adhered to by Spengler. Spengler's view of history claims to be elevated far above the narrow limitations of positivistic naturalism. He views culture not as the product of fixed physical factors but as the revelation of a fixed psychic domain [*Seelentum*], which is dependent upon nothing, which has no causal explanation, and which must be accepted as an irreducible fact. We cannot ask whence or from what a particular culture arose; for its birth is always a mystical act. A culture comes into being whenever an extraordinary soul suddenly "awakes from the primal soul-germinating state of eternally childlike humanity." Clearly this awakening is not meant to be described in terms of the concepts of natural science but is known only through inspiration. Hence, for Spengler, the true logic [*Organon*] of the philosophy of culture is not natural science but poetry. "To attempt to treat history with the methods of exact science," Spengler once remarked, "is always, in the final analysis, a contradiction in terms. . . . With regard to nature one must proceed scientifically, concerning history one must poetize." Thus we find him poetizing the epic of world history and the tragedy of the decline of

9. Concerning Comte's concept of *"Fatalité modifiable,"* cf. Ernst Troeltsch, *Der Historismus und seine Probleme, Gesammelte Schriften* (Tübingen: Mohr, 1912–25), III, 390 ff.

the West, just as he places before us in the mind's arena the
ranks of all the great cultures—the Apollonian, Arabic-
magic, the Faustian-Gothic. Each is completely self-con-
tained, comparable to no other, and intelligible through
no other; for each is the expression of a unique psychic
realm, which blooms and fades, never to return to that day
of glory. This mystical fate encapsules the individual being
and his every act far more tightly, and subjects him to a far
more rigid and inexorable necessity, than the "modifiable
fate" of naturalistic positivism. For here all possibility of
modification has vanished. The blooming and fading of
individual cultures is a decree of fate, which we can do
nothing to avert. We cannot seize the arm of fate; the
Wheel of Ixion to which we are chained cannot be retarded
nor can it be given a new direction. The "colossal course of
life" of each culture-soul completely engulfs the being and
will of the human individual; he can do nothing but sub-
mit to it as its prisoner and, in the face of it, take cognizance
of his own nothingness.

Hegel's philosophy of history appears to present a diametrically opposite interpretation. For Hegel's philosophy
purports to be a philosophy of freedom. And yet, the idea
of freedom in the metaphysical idealism which lies at the
base of the Hegelian system attributes the process of freedom only to the Infinite, only to the Absolute Subject, not
to the finite subject. The latter remains as strictly bound as
ever, for it is nothing but a moment in the world-event,
nothing but a means which the World Spirit utilizes to its
own end. The finite subject is only apparently the doer of
his acts; what he is and does he holds in fee from the Absolute Idea. For it is this which assigns to him his role and
marks out the sphere of his activities. Indeed, according to
Hegel, the "ultimate subtlety of reason" consists in the

very fact that it forever appears in the form of independence to the individual, completely seducing him with this deception, but without the least guarantee of actual independence. Absolute Reason utilizes the particular goals and passions of individuals, though not for the sake of these individuals, but as her own. Here, too, the individual is a mere marionette of the omnipotent, self-moving Idea. In believing we push, we are pushed; we are the instrument of a higher power, which directs us according to its own goals and to whose commands we willingly succumb.

In addition to this threefold combination of physics, psychology, and metaphysics, is there still another possible standpoint from which to gain leverage capable of guaranteeing independent significance and worth to the being and the actions of the individual?

I cannot attempt here to formulate axiomatically and systematically the answer to this question—a question which greets us at the starting point of any philosophy of culture. In the scope of this brief sketch, I must be content with an historical analysis. This cannot be done better nor more briefly than by calling to mind those men who not only conceived the ideal of a new "humanistic" basis for the study of culture, but who have realized it for us in their work and have thus breathed soul and life into it.

In the second half of the eighteenth century, in the period of classical German literature, a new humanism frees itself and begins to stand on its own feet; it has a totally different stamp and a far greater breadth and depth than Renaissance humanism. But even the humanism of the Renaissance was no mere scholarly movement; for it, too, in such great minds as Erasmus, embodied a universal educational and cultural ideal which resolutely encountered life head on. The battlecry, *"ad fontes,"* orients this hu-

manism toward the past and continues to hold it firmly
fixed upon it. The classicism of the eighteenth century is
of another kind. In spite of all the reverence and admira-
tion for antiquity which dominates it and gives it its stamp,
it is concerned far more with the future than with the past.
For here the differentiating motive is the desire to create,
not the desire to contemplate.

In its strictly philosophical motives, Herder's interpretation of history is rooted in the thinking of Leibniz. And,
for Leibniz, the present—insofar as it is regarded not as
physical existence but simply as what is genuinely present
to consciousness—always harbors a duplex moment. It is
"Chargé du passe et gros de l'avenir"; it is filled with the
past and pregnant with the future. This new dimension
which enters the reading of history can be detected in Herder's *Ideen* and in Lessing's *Education of the Human Race.*
But it is difficult to grasp and define, in purely conceptual
terms, the new doctrine of man, the new "historical appre-
ciation of man,"[10] at work here. This can only be had
within the texture of an intimate acquaintance with the
works of Winckelmann and Lessing, Herder and Schiller,
Goethe and Wilhelm von Humboldt. In a conversation
with Eckermann, Goethe once defended himself against
all attempts to give abstract expression to the common idea
running through the poetic picture of Faust. "If," he said,
"I were to attempt to string upon the meager thread of a
single all-comprehending idea so rich, many colored, and
complex a life as I have brought to perception in Faust, the
very act of doing so would of necessity become just such a

10. Goethe's term. Cf. "Maximen und Reflexionen," ed. Max
Hecker, *Schriften der Goethe-Gesellschaft* (Weimar: Goethe-Gesellschaft, 1927), XXI, 494.

thing of beauty."[11] Nor does that most complex of intellectual life running through the poetry and philosophy of German classical literature admit of being defined by one idea and one only. It is a mistake and quite misleading to attempt in all seriousness to find "that one incisive and elegant formula" by which to give expression to one's own intimate experience—as Taine, who loved such formulas, has done, and with masterful skill.

Instead, here one can only pursue the path of *indirect* description and *indirect* historical characterization. And, with this, a negative factor first makes its appearance. We are particularly habituated to studying the eighteenth century's "ideal conception of humanity" [*"Humanitätsideal"*] from an ethical point of view; we are accustomed to looking upon it, if not exclusively, at least for the most part as an ethical ideal. But this interpretation is clearly too narrow. For Winckelmann and Herder, for Goethe and Humboldt, indeed, even for Schiller and Kant, the truly concrete significance of this concept of humanity lies elsewhere. To be sure, they are convinced that a specific form of morality and a specific order of social and political life flow from the idea of *"humanitas"* and that, in a certain sense, these represent its ripest and noblest fruit. But this is not the only object of their vision. For, beyond this, they are confronting, in addition, a far more universal theme, a far more comprehensive problem.

What concerns them in the concept of humanity does not lie completely within the limits of the moral order. It extends to every creative act whatever, regardless of the particular sphere of life within which it realizes itself. Here

11. Conversation with Eckermann on May 6, 1827, ed. Flodard Friedrich von Biedermann, *Goethes Gespräche* (Leipzig, 1910), III, 394.

there emerges, as *the fundamental feature of all human existence,* the fact that man is not lost within the welter of his external impressions, that he learns to control this sea of impressions by giving it *ordered form,* which, as such, stems in the final analysis from himself, from his own thinking, feeling, and willing.

This desire and capacity for giving form to experience is what Herder and Humboldt show to be the essence of language, what Schiller points to as the essential nature of play and art, and what Kant shows us to be true of the structure of theoretical knowledge. For them, all this would not be possible as outgrowth, as sheer product, if unique modes of formal construction [spheres of possibility] did not underlie [the working out of] these creations. The very fact that man is capable of this type of productivity is precisely what stands out as the unique and distinguishing characteristic of human nature. *"Humanitas,"* in the widest sense of the word, denotes that completely universal—and, in this very universality, unique—medium in which "form," as such, comes into being and in which it can develop and flourish.

But the setting off of this special sphere [of human activity and cultural existence] in no way implies the assumption or the requirement that, to demonstrate and support it, we must go beyond the sphere of natural existence for our first principles. In a sense, the Kantian "Revolution concerning our modes of thought" does, in fact, demand such a leap, such a transcendence of our concepts of nature. Kant's doctrine rests upon a dualism between nature and freedom, between the *"mundus sensibilis"* and the *"mundus intelligibilis."* But Herder and Goethe have not followed him here. What they comprehend under the idea of *humanitas* they view not so much as a unique [state of] *be-*

ing, but, instead, as a unique *achievement.* Of all *natural beings* only man is capable of this achievement. "He can differentiate, select, and direct—he can impart duration to a moment." What the human being thus completes is the *objectification,* the apperception, of the ground of all theoretical, aesthetic, and ethical creation of form. It is present in the first utterance that is true speech, and it finds itself with ever increasing richness and subtlety in poetry, in visual art, in religious vision, in philosophical concept. All this gives expression to the unique capacity and industry of the human being, his *capacitas infinita,* if we may use Comenius' term. But this *capacitas infinita,* this orientation toward the infinite, implies at the same time a severe self-limitation. For all form demands a determinate mass and is bound to its sheer thereness. Life cannot produce form purely from itself, as naked, freely streaming activity; it must concentrate and focus, as it were, on a fixed point in order to take part in [the world of] form.

The philosophically correct presentation and grounding of this insight has not been achieved by the metaphysical systems of German idealism, although they, too, have continually touched upon the problem we are raising here and have sought its solution within the framework of their own presuppositions and concepts. It was not Fichte, Schelling, nor Hegel, but Wilhelm von Humboldt who succeeded in erecting this bridge [between nature and human nature]. It is impossible to gain a completely clear picture of the development of philosophic thought at the beginning of the nineteenth century if one follows only the course of development of the great systems. For in keeping to such a scheme of study, and it is the one which has continually dominated all presentation of the history of modern philosophy, we lose something important and essential to this development; we forfeit contemplation of an intellectual terrain which emerges at once in full clarity and significance in Humboldt's work.

To be sure, at first glance Humboldt's thought appears far less complete than that of Fichte, Schelling, or Hegel. The further he proceeds in his work the more he appears to lose himself in particular problems of scientific investigation and in the details of this research. But he brings a truly philosophical spirit to all of this and never loses sight of the whole within which these investigations have their meaning. All that Humboldt achieved as statesman, as political theorist, as philosopher of history, as aesthetician, and as pioneer in the philosophy of language can be subsumed under one germinal idea—that of an all-encompassing universalism which at the same time is and must continue to be the purest individualism. Here the limitations of Spinoza's thought, which strongly influenced Humboldt, emerge in full clarity. Spinoza's universalism is metaphysical in nature and derivation. He finds that it is necessary for the ego to undergo a self-renunciation if it is to have a vision of the whole, if it would participate in full knowledge of God and nature. Thus it holds also for each human personality that *"Omnis determinatio est negatio."* In its particularity and limitation, uniqueness of personality is the polar opposite of the infinite being of God and nature. Thus, to remain fixed and bound up in our uniqueness is necessarily to once again be in danger of anthropocentrism and anthropomorphism.

The neo-humanism of Goethe, Herder, and Humboldt calls for a different union. To them, the Spinozistic thesis, that definition is limitation, is valid only where it applies to external limitation, such as the form given to an object by a force not its own. But within the free sphere of one's personality such checking heightens personality; it truly acquires form only by forming itself. Consequently, though we are obliged to recognize in the definition of personality a limitation, when compared to the infinite being of God and nature, we are also obliged to acknowledge, and to come to know intimately, that this very shaping of one's personality is a genuine and underived power.

Every universal in the sphere of culture, whether discovered in language, art, religion, or philosophy, is as individual as it is universal. For in this sphere we perceive the universal only within the actuality of the particular; only in it can the cultural universal find its actualization, its realization as a cultural universal. Humboldt has developed this basic thesis with particular reference to language in the preface to his extensive work on the Kavi language. For him, language is "the clearest evidence and the surest proof that the human being does not possess a self-enclosed individuality; that the words 'I' and 'you' not only mutually support each other; that, as concepts, they are identical; and that, in this sense, there *is* a sphere of individuality, including the weak, needy, and perishing and extending back to the remotest beginnings of mankind." According to Humboldt, without such a rudimentary universality [in the concept "self"] all understanding of others, all human life within the medium of speech would be forever impossible. As historian and philosopher of history Humboldt held firmly to this fundamental insight and found new support and proof of it. All historical life is nationally conditioned and limited; but in this very conditioning, indeed, by virtue of it, it exemplifies the universality, the unbroken oneness, of the human race.

A nation . . . by virtue of its specific language, constitutes a mental style of human nature, hence individ-
ualized in relation to the idealized whole [of human
nature]. In all that moves the human breast, but especially in speech, there lives not only a striving
toward unity and universality but also an assumption,
indeed an inward conviction, that the human species,
in spite of all separation, all diversity, is still, in its
primal nature and its ultimate realization, inseparably
one. . . . Individuality separates off in the most remarkable manner, for it is in the very process of differentiation into greater individuality that this feeling of unity
awakens; indeed, it appears to be means to its realization; at least, in thought it proves to be so. . . . Deep
within, struggling toward that unity and universality
of mankind, the human being desires to transcend the
separating limitations of his individuality. To raise his
individual [and national] existence to this lofty sphere,
he must do precisely as the giant who received and
maintained his strength only by renewing contact with
his homeland.[12]

Even in his classicism Humboldt finds this trait. As he
puts it in his essay "On the Task of the Historian," "Greece
erected an idea of national unity such as the world had
never seen and has never seen since; and since the secret
of existence is individuality, so all advancement of mankind
throughout history goes no further than the mutual interplay of freedom and uniqueness."[13]

12. Humboldt, "Ueber die Verschiedenheit des menschlichen
Sprachbaues," *Gesammelte Schriften* (Berlin: Academy Edition, 1907),
VII, 125.
13. Humboldt, IV, 52 f.

None of the systems of historical determinism which we have studied has conceived the principle of individuality with such depth and clarity. To be sure, even a first impression of the thinkers of French positivism shows that their naturalism and determinism by no means preclude an understanding of individualism. All these thinkers are artists in too high a degree not to be individualists also. If as theorists they often find it difficult to acknowledge the unique worth of individuals, still, they are fully aware of its charm and succumb to it again and again, as if against their will. In fullest measure, they have the gift for aesthetically identifying with others, and for psychological analysis; and they employ these talents with the utmost subtlety in exploring and presenting the world of the mind and the emotions. In his large work, *Port Royal*, as well as in *Causeries du Lundi* and *Portraits littéraires,* Sainte-Beuve has produced a form and technique of literary portraiture, which has scarcely been equalled since, let alone surpassed.

And Taine, even by his doctrine of the omnipotence of "environment," does not mean that for the naturalistic historian history dissolves into nothing but matter in motion. He strives to make intelligible the cultural core of each of the ages he studies by studying specific individuals in all their concrete uniqueness. In the final analysis, he insists, there are neither mythologies nor languages; there are only human beings who use words and fashion images and concepts.

A dogma is nothing in itself; to understand it look at the men who made it, at this or that portrait of the sixteenth century, at the hard, energetic face of an archbishop or an English martyr. True history first emerges for us when the historian succeeds in taking

us across the barrier of time and face to face with living
human beings—human beings governed by distinctive
mannerisms, possessed of specific passions, having each
his own voice and physiognomy, his own gestures and
clothes, and with the same completeness and clarity
belonging to those human beings who walk our own
streets. . . . *Rien n'existe que par l'individu; c'est l'individu lui-même qu'il faut connaître.* . . . A language,
a legal code, a catechism, are forever mere abstractions;
the concrete, the genuinely real, is what can be handled, the bodily and visible human being, who eats,
works, and fights. Forget the theory of contracts and
their mechanisms, put aside the study of religion and
its systems and resolve instead to see the human being
at work, in his office, in his field, with his sunshine, his
soil, his shelter, his clothes, and his mealtime. This is
the first step in the study of history.[14]

It would seem that no keener nor more forthright ac-
knowledgment of individualism could be given than that
which is presented here. But, in the end, what is the individual for Taine and where are we to look for the core of
his being? For him, it no longer lies, as it did for the humanism of the seventeenth and eighteenth centuries, in a
"monadic" being, in the "imprinted form which in living
unfolds itself." Instead, it lies in the physical-psychic material, in the fundamental *drive*, which, in the same act,
dominates, and is claimed by, the individual. Once we have
grasped this basic drive, we have that human being before
us in his totality, with all his representations and thoughts,
his ideas and ideals. For, looked at from the standpoint of

14. Taine, *Histoire de la Littérature Anglaise,* pp. v ff.

biogeny, man is and can be nothing more than a higher species of animal—an animal producing a poem or a philosophical system with the same necessity by which the silkworm produces its cocoon and the bee its combs.

What we have said of the individual in Taine's philosophy applies to the concept of the "culture-soul" in Spengler's philosophy of history. As Taine puts it, our mind is as mathematically constructed as a piece of clockwork; likewise for Spengler, the "culture-soul," in spite of the romantic and mythical aura which surrounds it, is a mechanism, whose movement we can predict to the minutest detail once we understand its motive principle. Human individuals are completely enmeshed in this wheelwork. Their independent creative power is mere illusion. For, according to Spengler, it is a mistake to think that German culture, for example, would have acquired a different pattern and taken a different course if Goethe or Beethoven had died in childhood. The life-event of the "culture-soul" would not be altered; for with their disappearance, what was to have been their achievement would be done "by other heads replacing them."

It is of considerable systematic and cultural-historical interest to observe how, in the interpretation of history, two motives, which appear to be diametrically opposite in meaning and origin, can be welded together. Hegel's philosophy of history sees in freedom the truly great theme of world history and it defines the latter as "progress in the consciousness of freedom." Thus, the orientals have "known only that *one* is free, the Greco-Roman world that only *a few* are free; the fact that *each of us* is aware that every man, i.e., man as man, is free, is itself the unfolding of world history. Philosophy teaches us that all intellectual qualities have their being only in a state of freedom, that

all are but means at the disposal of freedom, that all their
striving and creating is simply for the sake of freedom; it
is the one knowledge peculiar to speculative philosophy
that the one thing uniquely a property of the mind is freedom."[15] But Hegel demands that philosophy do more than
merely assert this thesis, that it prove it. And he insists that
it can be proved only by means of the dialectic method,
through the logical necessity inherent in this method. According to him, Kant and Fichte were unable to furnish
proof of this thesis regarding the freedom of the mind. For
them, freedom remains simply an ideal which, left as such,
they condemned to the "impotence of the mere ought." In
order to succeed in getting from "ought" to "is," in order,
once and for all, to reconcile idea and reality, it must be
shown that the real is rational and the rational real. In
spite of the gulf which French naturalism had put between
itself and the basic presuppositions of the Hegelian system,
it had by no means turned away from its *methodological*
presuppositions. Though the thinkers of this school took
the working ideas of their research and their science from
the doctrines of Comte, the Hegelian logic and phenomenology had also had a strong influence on them.

Taine has told us that the reading of Hegel's *Logic* belongs among the decisive events of his youth, and he adds
that he spent six months digesting this monster.[16] In spite
of his thoroughgoing empiricism, he never ceased to be inspired by the hope of reducing the factual and the contin-
gent to the necessary, *"de passer de l'accidentel au néces-*

15. Hegel, *Sämtliche Werke* (Stuttgart: F. Frommann, 1927–40),
IX, 22 ff.
16. Taine, *Vie et Correspondance* (Paris, 1903–1907), II, 30; cf. also
Babbitt, *The Masters of Modern French Criticism* (New York: Houghton Mifflin Company, 1912), pp. 224 ff.

saire, du relatif à l'absolu, de l'apparence à la vérité."[17] According to Taine, this can no longer be left to speculative philosophy; this was the overriding task to which empirical science must address itself; and he believed its fulfillment and realization by the nineteenth century sciences to be imminent. Even in his youthful work *L'Avenir de la Science* Renan had given expression to the hope that this achievement was near at hand. Science would fulfill what religion had promised but had been incapable of fulfilling. It would create a new humanity and secure the peace and happiness of mankind. But this was written before Renan had rubbed shoulders with the actual state of science. It is a picture of the enthusiastic prospect which this twenty-five-year-old saw dawning before him. But the more Renan advanced, the more he delved into his work as philologist and critical historian of myth and religion, the deeper the shadows that began to fall across this vision. He begins to ask whether science, too, has not failed, if we expect ethical and not merely theoretical things of it—if we hope to use it not merely as the instrument of knowledge but as the true organon for transforming human life. He continually refuses to give in to this thought; but this very persistence causes him to lose heart. As he remarks in one of his journals, "The religious man lives for a shadow; but we live for the shadow of a shadow: what will those who come after us live for?"[18]

Here a break in naturalism's view of life and its ideal of science suddenly looms into view. This new question becomes increasingly disturbing—the question *"De quoi vivra-t-on après nous?"* It is evident from this that Comte was

17. *Histoire de la Littérature Anglaise*, V, 410.
18. Cf. Walter Küchler, *Ernest Renan, Der Dichter und der Künstler* (Gotha, 1921), p. 195.

lucky enough to find sustenance here only by virtue of the fact that he envisaged a new positivistic and sociocratic religion and sought to introduce a new cult, the cult of the *"Grand Être."* But in doing so he was already abandoning his own methodology; he had embarked upon a μετάβασις εἰς ἄλλο γένος. To attempt to avoid taking this step, to hold strictly to positivism and naturalism, is to become increasingly disillusioned with that initial optimistic hope.

None of the adherents to French naturalism is totally free of this note of skepticism. Although they all feel that "nothing can disturb" the enthusiasm which permeates and animates their scientific work, in practical matters they must resolve to be resigned. Sainte-Beuve once remarked that basically he was a melancholy skeptic unsure even of his own doubt.[19] Taine is far more decisive and doctrinaire, but even as an historian he has not denied having this reservation. Even his historical masterpiece, *Les Origines de la France contemporaine,* is far from making good that methodological ideal which he had projected for it. Nowhere does it succeed in handling questions of virtue and vice as if they were comparable to the analysis of sulphuric acid or sugar. Indeed, he declares in the Preface that the historian is to proceed exactly as the natural scientist. He sought, without reservation, to study and describe the political development of France just as one would the metamorphosis of an insect.[20] Nevertheless, if we abandon ourselves to his treatment, we continually feel a passionate participation in the events which he depicts. Instead of merely describing and explaining them in terms of their ultimate causes—in terms of race, place, and time—Taine

19. Cf. Babbitt, *op. cit.,* p. 111.
20. Taine, *Les Origines de la France contemporaine,* 12th ed. (Paris: Librairie Hachette, 1882), p. v.

scrutinizes, arranges, evaluates, and judges as to right and wrong. But such psychological and historical judgment is far from achieving that Hegelian picture of world history in which *"Idee"* [the rational thought process] is supposed to be the true, the eternal, the all-conquering. How can we believe here in the triumph of reasoning, how can we not see that the historical process is determined through hard realities of a totally different nature and a totally different origination? For here we find nothing but empirical man, who cannot belie his nature.

So it is that Taine admits we must give up the dream of "perfectability." And as for the essential and distinctive traits of human nature, psychology and history show us only a perfect stability, unaltered by any supposed advance of culture. The appearance of human "wisdom" evaporates; what we call wisdom is never more than a lucky product of favorable circumstances. Thus it is by no means the rule, but the exception, *"une rencontre,"* as Taine himself once summed it up. The character of the human race as a whole is untouched and unaltered by such "accidental hits." Naturalism began with the Faustian craving for knowledge, with an apotheosis of knowledge as the one factor capable of bringing about man's salvation. But the belief that science is not only capable of understanding human nature, that it is also called upon to cure its evils and shortcomings, continues to fade as these representatives of naturalism, as historians and psychologists, probe deeper and deeper into the depths of this nature. As Taine puts it in his sketch of the realistic art of Fielding,

> Ce qu'on appelle nature c'est cette couvée de passions secrètes, souvent malfaisantes, ordinairement vulgaires, toujours aveugles, qui frémissent et frétil-

lent en nous, mal recouvertes par le manteau de dé-
cence et de raison sous lequel nous tâchons de les dé-
guiser; nous croyons les mener, elles nous mènent;
nous nous attribuons nos actions, elles les font. Il y en
a tant, elles sont si fortes, si entrelacées les unes dans
les autres, si promptes à s'éveiller, à s'élancer et à s'en-
traîner, que leur mouvement échappe à tous nos rai-
sonnements et à toutes nos prises.[21]

Here we no longer find even a trace of the Hegelian view
of history. We hear only the wisdom of Schopenhauer and
Mephistopheles: "The little World-God stays always on the
same beat and is just as strange as on that first day."[22]

At bottom, what we have encountered here is a crisis in
the *concept of evolution* upon which the entire naturalistic philosophy of culture is built. The dialectical meaning
of evolution presented in Hegel's system leaves no doubt
but that all evolution is directed toward a single and highest goal, the realization of the "Absolute Idea." This teleological enclosure does not disappear when the concept of
evolution sheds its idealistic stamp and emerges in purely
empirical and naturalistic form. For of Comte and Spencer
it is also true that nature itself stands subject to the laws of
progress, of differentiation, and integration. Spencer's doctrine of evolution, as Troeltsch has correctly said, "is the
perfect mirror-image in empirical form of Schelling's dialectic taken in the first phase of its influence as mediated
through Coleridge—the dialectic of the upward thrust of
life toward increasing individuality in the face of increasing
organization—and translated by him into what he felt to

21. Taine, *Histoire de la Littérature Anglaise,* IV, 130.
22. "Der kleine Gott der Welt bleibt stets von gleichem Schlag
Und ist so wunderlich als wie am ersten Tag."

be the self-evident thought modes of positivistic naturalism."[23] Spencer himself appears to have been oblivious to
the dualism which lies concealed in his concept of evolution; for, in spite of all his empiricism and agnosticism, in
the basic features of his system he remains a "naïve" metaphysician. But a critical examination of these basic assumptions of biological knowledge necessarily leads us beyond
these conclusions and presents us with new problems. It
shows us that a causal theory of evolution is little proof of
any advance in human nature and human history. For if we
strictly abide by the demands of scientific objectivity, a
searching examination of these assumptions forces us to
resignation [as regards this naïve belief in an evolution in
human nature]; it is a resignation which our own scientific
thinking imposes upon us and it will necessarily be one of
disillusionment if we have set out with such exuberant ex-
pectations.

And what are we to conclude from all of this? Are we to
be disgusted with science because it has not fulfilled our
hopes or redeemed its promises? And are we, for this reason, to announce the "bankruptcy" of science, as is so often
and so flippantly done? But this is rash and foolish; for we
can hardly blame science just because we have not asked the
right questions. And it is surely a false formulation of the
problem and a mistaken expectation to demand of science
that it not only bring us to clearer and more precise knowledge of the laws of objective reality but, in addition, fore-
tell the future of human culture, including, of course, the
future of natural science itself. We must admit and confess
that such predetermination is possible neither empirically
and inductively nor by dialectical and speculative means.

23. Troeltsch, *Der Historismus und seine Probleme,* III, 421.

But it is not only in the domain of cultural events that such "predetermination" has become problematic, the same must now be said of knowledge of natural events. Here, too, we have more and more abandoned the ideal of complete prediction in the sense of the Laplacean mind. This is not to say that we have abandoned the concept of causality; however, it has assumed a different and epistemologically unobjectionable meaning.[24] But even on the basis of classical physics, critically minded physicists, like Helmholtz, have insisted that we can neither require nor expect *proof* of causal statements from the natural scientist; for every empirical proof—and this could only be a piece of natural research—necessarily involves us in a vicious circle. But, according to Helmholtz, this does not prevent the advance of natural science. Here only one admonition is sound: "Believe and act!" Empirical research must assume the concept of causality as its immanent regulative principle and look for its substantiation and guarantee in the extent to which its development yields ever richer concrete empirical results.[25]

If this is true of physics, it is true of the humanities in an even stricter and more telling sense. We are incapable of anticipating the future development of civilization. Nor can it be completely understood through any amount of empirical knowledge of its past and present. Nor can philosophy transcend these limits to our empirical knowledge. As critical philosophy, it endeavors to understand the universal and basic cultural orientations; it seeks, above all, to

24. For further discussion of this see my *Determinism and Indeterminism in Modern Physics*.

25. Hermann von Helmholtz, *Die Tatsachen in der Wahrnehmung* (1878) and *Vorträge and Reden*, 4th ed. (Braunschweig: F. Vieweg und Sohn, 1896) p. 244.

penetrate to an understanding of the universal principles according to which man "gives structure" to his experience.

But even this is no basis for prophecy; least of all where it concerns itself not simply with physical being and happening but with human action. Human action is known only in its realization; only when realized are we aware of its living possibilities. Prior to its realization it is not restricted to a fixed and clearly delimited sphere of possibilities; indeed, its work is precisely that of seeking and creating ever new possibilities. This seeking and creating is the achievement of the truly great, the truly productive individuals.

The continually erupting anxiety over the destiny and future of human civilization can hardly be prevented by a critical philosophy of culture. It, too, must recognize this barrier to historical determinism or prediction. All that can be said on this score is that culture will advance just to the extent that the truly creative powers, which in the final analysis are only brought into play by our own efforts, are not forsaken or crippled. This one prediction we can make, and for ourselves, for our own actions and decisions, its certainty is of unique and supreme importance. To be sure, it does not give us unqualified certainty in advance that we will achieve specific goals; what it does show us is the necessity of our own subjective response in the face of these goals. And, with this, our very not-knowing achieves, not only a negative, but also a positive and decisive significance.

In his philosophy of history Hegel sought to provide the ultimate speculative proof that reason is omnipotent substance. In place of this, we must remember his insight that *reason* is "not so impotent as to pass for a mere ideal, a mere ought." The critique at the beginning of the Hegelian system has pulled the ground from under *that* mode of

argument. And if we return from the Hegelian notion of
idea to the Kantian, from idea as "absolute power" to idea
as "infinite problem," we must, of course, give up the speculative optimism of the Hegelian view of history. But, by
doing so, we also give up fatalistic pessimism with its proph-
ecies and visions of decline. With this, human action
again has an open opportunity to determine itself by its
own power and through its own answers, knowing full well
that the direction and future of civilization are dependent
upon this kind of determination.

THE LOGIC OF THE HUMANITIES

CHAPTER 1

The Subject Matter
of the Humanities

PLATO HAS SAID that the true philosophic emotion is wonder and that in it we see the root of all philosophizing. If
that be true, the question arises as to which objects first
awakened wonder in man and thus set him upon the road of
philosophic reflection. Were these objects "physical" or
"spiritual"? Was it the order of nature or man's own creations which here took precedence?

As a working assumption, it would appear that the astronomical world was the first to rise out of chaos. We encounter veneration for the stars in nearly all great civilized
religions. Here man was first able to free himself from the
brooding thrall of feeling and to raise himself to a freer and
wider vision of the whole of existence. That subjective passion which strives to exercise control through magical powers began to recede; the inkling of a universal order was beginning to stir in its place. In the coursing of the stars, in
the alternation of night and day, in the orderly return of
the seasons, man found his first great example of a uniform
occurrence. This occurrence was elevated infinitely far
above his own sphere and removed from his volitions and
wishes. It retained nothing of that caprice and incalculabil-

ity which characterizes, not only ordinary human action, but also the operation of "primitive" demonic powers. That there is an operation [*Wirken*], and hence a reality [*Wirklichkeit*] enclosed within fixed limits and bound by determinate and unalterable laws—this was the insight which here began to dawn for the first time.

But this sentiment immediately began to link itself to another. Far closer to man than the order of nature stands the order which he finds in that world which is peculiarly his own. Here, too, it is by no means mere arbitrary will that governs. The individual sees himself determined and limited from his first movements by something over which he has no power. It is the power of custom which binds him; it keeps watch over his every step, and it allows scarcely a moment of free play. Not only his actions, but also his feelings and representations, his beliefs and fancies are governed by it. Custom is the abiding, unaltering atmosphere in which he lives and has his being; he can no more remove himself from it than from the air he breathes. It is little wonder, then, that in his thoughts the vision of the physical world cannot free itself from that of the moral world. These two visions belong together and are one in their origin.

In their cosmogonies and moral teachings all great religions have based themselves on this theme. They are unanimous in attributing to the Creator a double role and a twofold task—to be the founder of the astronomical and moral order and to rescue both from the forces of Chaos. In the *Gilgamesh Epic,* in the *Vedas,* in the Egyptian creation story, we find the same vision. In the Babylonian creation myth we see Marduk waging battle against shapeless Chaos, against the monstrous Tiamat. Following his victory he erects those eternal monuments of the cosmic and moral orders: he determines the course of the stars; he establishes the signs of the zodiac; he fixes the succession of days, months, and years. And at the same time he sets limits to human action, limits which cannot be transgressed with impunity. It is he who "sees into the innermost depths, who does not allow the evildoer to escape, who curbs the disobedient and causes justice to prevail."[1]

But this miracle of the moral order is linked to others no less august and mysterious. For all that man creates and brings forth with his own hands still surrounds him as an incomprehensible mystery. When he contemplates his own works he is far from suspecting himself as their creator. They stand far above him; they are elevated not only above the individual but above all that the human species can achieve. If man ascribes an origin to them, it can only be a mythical one. A god created them; a savior brought them down from heaven to earth and taught man their use. Such culture-myths permeate the mythologies of all peoples and ages.[2] What the technical ingenuity of man has produced in the course of centuries and millennia are not deeds achieved by him but are talents and gifts from on high. For every tool there is such a supernatural origin. Among many primitive peoples as, for example, even today among the Ewe in South-Togoland, with the yearly return of the harvest celebration, offerings are made to each of the various tools— the ax, the plane, the saw.[3]

The intellectual tools which man has created he can only contemplate from a distance even more remote than that

1. For further details see my *Philosophy of Symbolic Forms,* trans. Ralph Manheim (New Haven: Yale University Press, 1955), II, 112 ff.

2. Cf. the material of Kurt Breysig, *Die Entstehung des Gottesgedankens und der Heilbringer* (Berlin: G. Bondi, 1905).

3. Cf. Jakob Spieth, *Die Religion der Eweer in Süd-Togo* (Leipzig: J. C. Hinrichs, 1911), p. 8.

from which he looks upon his material tools. They, too, are held to be the manifestation of a power infinitely superior to his own. This holds, above all, for speech and writing—the precondition of all human intercourse and community. A special and favored place in the hierarchy of divine powers is always the prerogative of the god from whose hands writing has come into being. In Egypt the moon-god Thoth appears at one and the same time as the "scribe among the gods" and as the judge of heaven. It is he who allows gods and men to know what is their due; for he determines the measure of things.[4] Speech and writing are valued as the origin of measure; for the capacity to fix the fleeting and changing, and thereby to remove the accidental and capricious, inheres, above all, in them.

In all this we already detect the feeling that in the sphere of myth and religion human culture is not something given and self-evident, but that it is a kind of miracle that requires explanation. But this first leads to a deeper self-awareness when man not only feels himself obliged and warranted in posing such questions but goes beyond this to the construction of an authentic and independent "method" by which he can *answer* them. This step was first taken in Greek philosophy: it is just this that makes it the great turning point in intellectual history. Here for the first time there is revealed that new power which alone can lead to a science of nature and a science of human civilization. In place of the unrestricted multiplicity of the mythical attempts at explanation, which focus on first one phenomenon and then another, there emerges the representation of a thoroughgoing unity of being, which must correspond to a similar unity of explanation. This unity is accessible only to pure thought.

4. Cf. Alexandre Moret, *Mystères Egyptiens* (Paris: A. Colin, 1913), pp. 132 ff.

The diverse and numerous creations of the mythmaking imagination were henceforth rejected and eradicated by the critique of thought.

But a new and positive task is linked to this critical task. From its own powers and its own answers thought must rebuild what it has destroyed. In the systems of the Pre-Socratics we can trace the admirable consistency with which this task was attacked and carried through step by step. It found solution in Plato's theory of ideas and in Aristotle's metaphysics, which, for centuries, remained decisive and exemplary. Such a synthesis would not have been possible if a singleness of effort had not preceded it. Many tendencies contributed to it, tendencies which seem at first to be diametrically opposed; and they proceed in a variety of ways in the statement and solution of the problem. Still, if we look at it in terms of its origin and goal, this whole colossal labor of thought, in a certain measure, yields to being comprehended within *one* fundamental concept, which Greek philosophy was the first to discover and which it worked out and perfected in all its factors. In the development of Greek thought the concept which played this role was that of *logos*.[5]

The import and latent richness of the logos-concept can already be traced in the initial expression which it received in the philosophy of Heraclitus. At first glance the doctrine of Heraclitus still appears to stand wholly on the ground of Ionian natural philosophy. Heraclitus also sees the world as a totality of materials which reciprocally metamorphose

5. I have pursued this interpretation at greater length in the presentation of early Greek philosophy which I gave in Dessoir's *Lehrbuch der Philosophie* (Berlin: Ullstein, 1925), I, 7–135. Cf. also my article, "Logos, Dike, Kosmos in der Entwicklung der griechischen Philosophie," *Göteborgs Högskolas Arsskrift*, XLIII (1941: 6), 1–31.

into one another. But this appears to him only as the surface of events, beneath which there is a depth which he seeks to make visible, and which till now has not been disclosed to thought. The Ionians, too, are not to be satisfied with mere knowledge of the "what"; they also ask for the "how" and the "why." But this question is posed by Heraclitus with a new and far more precise meaning. And in giving the statement of the problem this new form, he is aware that perception, which is the sphere in which speculative natural philosophy has moved till now, is no longer capable of supplying the answer. Only *thought* can give us the answer: for in it, and it alone, is man freed of the limitations of his own individuality. He no longer pursues his "subjective understanding," but comprehends one that is universal and divine. A universal law [of the world] replaces the ἰδίη φρόνησις, "private insight." It is by so doing that man, according to Heraclitus, first frees himself from the mythical world of dream[s] and from the narrow and limited world of sense perception. For just this is the character of being awake and of awakened being—that individuals possess a common world, whereas in dream[s] each lives only in his own world and remains mired and imprisoned in it.

Here a new task was posed for the whole of Western thought, and with it a new direction was imparted, from which henceforth it was impossible ever to deviate. From the time this thought first permeated the school of Greek philosophy, all knowledge of reality was bound, to a certain extent, by this basic concept of *"logos"*—hence by "logic" in the widest sense. This direction was not altered when philosophy was pushed aside from its position of dominance and the "universal and divine" was sought at a different point, inaccessible to philosophy.

Christianity has struggled against Greek intellectualism.

But it is not able, and it does not wish, to return to mere
irrationalism. For the logos-concept has also become deeply
implanted in it. The history of Christian dogmatics shows
the persistent struggle which the fundamental impulse of
its religion of salvation has directed against the spirit of
Greek philosophy. Viewed as intellectual history, there is,
in this struggle, neither victor nor vanquished. Nor was
the struggle ever able to issue in an effective compromise
of opposites. The attempt to bring the logos-concept and
the Johannine gospel under *one* denominator [*Nenner*]
will always remain abortive. For within these two the manner of mediation between individual and universal, finite
and infinite, man and God, is radically different.

The Greek concept of being and the Greek concept of
truth are to be compared, according to the simile of Parmenides, to a "well-rounded sphere," whose support is its
own center. Both are complete in themselves and self-enclosed; and between them there obtains not only a harmony
but a true identity. The dualism of the Christian world
view brings this identity to an end.

Henceforth no effort of knowledge or of pure thought is
able to heal the rift which runs through being. To be sure,
Christian philosophy had in no sense abandoned the tendency toward unity, which lay in the concept of philosophy.
The more its failures at resolving the tension between these
polar opposites, the more it seeks to compromise them
within its own sphere and with its own means of thought.
All the great systems of scholastic philosophy grew out of
such attempts. None of them dares to contest the opposition
which persists between revelation and reason, between faith
and knowledge, between the *regnum gratiae* and the *regnum naturae*. Reason, i.e., philosophy, cannot construct a
unified view of nature from its own powers; all illumina-

tion of which it is capable stems not from itself but from a higher source of light. But, if it keeps its gaze directed to this source, if, instead of opposing an unaided and spontaneous power to faith, it allows itself to be guided and directed by the latter, then it will reach its allotted goal. The ultimate power of faith, which can come to man only through an immediate act of grace, through divine *"illuminatio,"* determines for him both the content and the limits of knowledge. In this sense the term *fides quaerens intellectum* becomes the epitome and motto of the whole of medieval Christian philosophy.

In the systems of high-scholasticism, especially in Thomas Aquinas, it might appear that the synthesis had been achieved and the lost harmony restored. "Nature" and "grace," "reason" and "revelation," do not contradict each other; rather, the one points to and calls for the other. The cosmos of culture appears again to be unified and tied to a firm religious center.

But this artfully dovetailed structure of scholasticism, in which Christian faith and ancient philosophical knowledge are required reciprocally to support and to maintain each other, collapses before that new ideal of knowledge which more than any other feature of modern science has determined and characterized it. The *mathematical science of nature* returns to the ancient ideal of knowledge. Kepler and Galileo are able to proceed directly from basic Pythagorean, Democritean, and Platonic concepts. But, at the same time, in their research, these concepts take on a new meaning. For they are capable of forming a bridge between the intelligible and the sensuous, between the κόσμος νοητός and the κοσμος ὁρατός, which was always lacking in ancient science and philosophy. The last boundaries between the "world of sense" and the "world of understanding" appeared to fall before mathematical knowledge. Matter itself seems to be pervaded by the harmony of number and subject to the lawfulness of geometry. Before this universal order all those opposites which had acquired fixity in Aristotelian and scholastic physics vanish. There is no contrast of "lower" and "higher," the world "above" and the world "below." The world is one as assuredly as *knowledge of the world* is one; for the world-mathematic is and can only be one.

This fundamental idea of modern [scientific] research found its decisive philosophical legitimation in Descartes' concept of *mathesis universalis*. The cosmos of universal mathematics, the cosmos of order and measure, comprehends and exhausts all knowledge. In itself it is completely autonomous; it requires no support and could recognize none, other than that which it finds within itself. Now, for the first time, reason comprehends the whole of being in its clear and distinct ideas; and now, for the first time, it is able to penetrate and dominate this whole by means of its own powers.

That this fundamental idea of classical philosophical rationalism not only fertilized and extended science, but that it gave to science a wholly new meaning and goal—this requires no detailed presentation. The development of systems of philosophy from Descartes to Malebranche and Spinoza, and from Spinoza to Leibniz affords unbroken evidence of this. In it we have direct testimony as to how ever new spheres of our knowledge were conquered as the new ideal of a universal mathematics developed. What is decisive in Descartes' system of metaphysics is his original conception of a single all-inclusive method of knowledge— with the one exception that thought, in the progress of its movement, will be led to distinct and radical differences within being which it can only acknowledge and accept as such.

The *dualism of substances* qualifies the *monism of* the Cartesian *method* and sets fixed limits to it. Ultimately, it would appear that the goal which this method sets for itself is not attainable for knowledge of reality as a whole, but only for determinate aspects of it. Without qualification, the corporeal world yields to the sway of mathematical thought. In it there is no inconceivable remainder; there are no dark "qualities," which are independent and irreducible, in contrast to the pure concepts of magnitude and number. All this is put aside and extinguished: the identity of "matter" and pure extension assures the identity of natural philosophy and mathematics. But next to extended substance there stands thinking substance; and, finally, both must be deduced from a common and ultimate ground—from the being of God. When Descartes proceeds beyond this point—to prove and lay bare this ultimate reach of reality—he abandons the guiding thread of his method. Here he no longer thinks in the concepts of his universal mathematics, but in the concepts of medieval ontology. For him, the proof can succeed only if he presupposes the validity of these concepts—if he begins with their "objective" existence—in order, then, to draw conclusions regarding the "formal" reality of things.

Descartes' successors are forever energetically and successfully attempting to remove this contradiction [in method]. They strive to accomplish for *substantia cogitans* and for the divine Substance what Descartes has achieved for *substantia extensa,* and in an equally convincing manner. It is in this way that Spinoza is led to his positing of God and nature as one and the same. And it is in this manner that Leibniz arrives at his sketch of a "universal characteristic."

Both are convinced that full proof of the truth of pan-logicism and pan-mathematicism can only be brought about in this way. Here the contour of the modern view of the world stands out against the ancient and medieval visions with the utmost sharpness and distinctness. "Spirit" and "reality" are not only reconciled to each other; they have interpenetrated one another. Between them there stands no relation of mere external influence or of external correspondence. Here it is no longer a question of that *adequatio intellectus et rei,* which ancient as well as scholastic epistemology had posited as the criterion of knowledge. It is a question of a pre-established harmony, of an ultimate identity between thought and being, between the ideal and the real.

The initial *limitation* which the pan-mathematical vision of the world encountered stems from a complex of problems which, as yet, was scarcely realized as such, or which was seen only in its incipient outlines. The second half of the eighteenth century was the first to set forth this new and great divide, as it came more and more to recognize its true form, and finally pushed it into the very center of philosophic awareness. Classical rationalism had not contented itself with the conquest of nature; it had sought also to construct a self-enclosed "scientific system of the nature of spirit." The human spirit was to cease to be a "state within a state"; it was to be known by the same principles, and the same lawfulness was to underlie it that underlies nature. Modern natural law, as founded by Hugo Grotius, appeals to the thoroughgoing analogy which obtains between knowledge of law and mathematical knowledge; Spinoza creates a new form of ethics, which orients itself by taking geometry as its pattern and sets itself to the imitation of both its goal [unconditioned knowledge] and its method. Here, for the first time, the sphere [of knowledge] appears

to be complete; the circle of mathematical thought has
been able to encompass, with the same method, the world of
matter and the world of the soul, the being of nature and
the being of history. But it is just on this last point that
fundamental doubt begins to set in for the first time. Is
history capable of the same mathematizing as physics or
astronomy? Is it nothing but a particular instance of
mathesis universalis?

The first philosopher to raise this question with true precision was Giambatista Vico. The real value of Vico's "philosophy of history" does not lie in what it teaches (in terms
of content) concerning the historical process and the rhythm
of its individual phases. This distinction of the epochs of
human history and the attempt to demonstrate a determinate law of succession, a transition from "divine" to "heroic,"
from "heroic" to "human"—all this is still interfused in
Vico with purely fantastic features. But what he did see
clearly, and what he defended with complete decisiveness
against Descartes, was the methodological uniqueness and
the distinctive value of historical knowledge. Nor is he slow
in elevating this value above that of pure mathematical
knowledge and in finding in it the first true fulfillment of
that *sapientia humana,* which Descartes had erected as an
ideal in the opening sentences of his *Regulae ad direction-
em ingenii.*

According to Vico, the true goal of our knowledge is not
knowledge of nature but human self-knowledge. If, instead
of restricting itself to this, philosophy claims divine and
absolute knowledge, it oversteps its limits and allows itself
to be enticed into a dangerous error. For Vico, the highest
law of knowledge is the statement that any being truly con-
ceives and fathoms only that which it itself has *produced.*
The sphere of our knowledge extends no further than the

sphere of our activity [*Schaffens*]. Man understands only insofar as he is creative; and strictly speaking this condition is attained, not in nature, but only in the world of spirit. Nature is the work of God and accordingly is completely intelligible only to that divine understanding which brought it forth. What man can truly conceive is not the essence of things, which for man is never completely exhaustible, but the structure and specificity of his own works. Even mathematics owes the clarity and certainty it possesses to this circumstance. For it is not grounded in physically real objects through mere imitation, but in ideal objects which thought has produced through free projection. But obviously this at once defines the limits of its value, limits which it cannot overstep. The objects of mathematics possess no other being than that abstract being which the human mind has endowed them with.

Hence the unavoidable alternative which our knowledge faces: it can orient itself toward the real, but in this case it can never completely penetrate its object, but describes it instead only piecemeal and empirically, with respect to particular properties and characteristics; or it can achieve complete insight, an adequate idea, which constitutes the nature and essence of the object, but then knowledge never leaves the sphere of its own concept formation. In the latter case, the object possesses only that structure which knowledge has ascribed to it by virtue of its arbitrary definition. According to Vico, we escape from this dilemma only when we go beyond the sphere of mathematical knowledge, and that of the knowledge of nature.

Thus the works of human *civilization* are the only ones which unite both conditions, and of which complete knowledge is possible. They have not only a conceivable but a completely determinate, individual, and historical exist-

ence. The inner structure of this existence is accessible and
open to the human mind because the human mind is its
creator. Myth, language, religion, poetry—these are the
objects to which human knowledge is truly commensurable.
And it is above all to these that Vico turns his gaze in constructing his "logic." Here for the first time logic dared to
break through the circle of objective knowledge, the circle
of mathematics and natural science, and dared instead to
constitute itself as the logic of the humanities—as the logic
of language, poetry, and history.

It is with good reason that Vico's *Scienza nuova* bears
its title. For it contains a truly original discovery. To be
sure, this originality is revealed less in the solutions which
the work offers than in the problems which it raises. Vico
was denied the privilege of laying bare the treasure hidden
in these problems. It was Herder who first raised into the
light of philosophic awareness what Vico had left in half-
mythical twilight. But Herder, likewise, is not a strictly
systematic thinker. His relation to Kant shows how unsympathetic he is to a "critique of knowledge" in the strict
sense. He does not care to analyze; his desire is to show.
He holds all knowledge to be vacuous which is not thoroughly determinate and concrete, and saturated with intuitive content. Nevertheless, Herder's work is important
not only for its content and not only for its new insights into
the philosophy of language, the theory of art, and the philosophy of history; at the same time, we are able to study
in it the rise and ultimate breakthrough of a new *form* of
knowledge, which, to be sure, is not to be abstracted from
its matter, but which becomes manifest only in the free
shaping of this matter and in its spiritual domination and
penetration.

Just as Vico had opposed Descartes' universal mathematic

and the mechanism of his view of nature, so Herder opposes the scholastic system of Wolff and the abstract culture of the intellect so dominant in the age of enlightenment. What he struggles against is the tyrannical dogmatism of this age, which is obliged to debase and suppress all of man's other spiritual and intellectual possibilities. Against this tyranny he invokes that radical maxim which was first instilled in him by his teacher Hamann: whatever man is required to perform must spring from the condensation and unbroken unity of all his powers; all that is isolated is evil.

In the first stages of his philosophy this unity is seen by Herder as an historical fact, standing at the threshold of human history. It is, for him, a lost paradise from which man has alienated himself more and more with the progress of his much lauded civilization. Only poetry in its oldest and original form still preserves for us a remembrance of this paradise. Accordingly, it is treasured by Herder as the true "mother tongue of the human race"—just as Hamann and Vico had treasured it. It is in poetry that he seeks to realize and make live again that original unity which, in the beginnings of historical language and myth, had fashioned history and poetry into a genuine totality, into an unpartitioned whole.

But the further Herder advances along his way the more he overcomes this Rousseauistic yearning for the "primitive" and original. In the final form which his philosophy of history and culture attained in the *Ideen,* the goal of totality no longer lies behind us. As a result, the whole accent of his doctrine is altered. For the differentiation of the powers of the spirit is no longer regarded simply as a deterioration of the original unity, as a kind of fall of knowledge into a state of sin; instead, it has attained a positive meaning and value. The true unity is that which

this separation presupposes and which is only regained
through it. All concrete spiritual events, all genuine "history" is only the reflection [*Bild*] of this continually renewing process, this "systole" and "diastole," this separation
and reintegration. Only after Herder had raised himself
to this universal conception could the individual factors
within the spiritual process attain for him their true independence and autonomy. Henceforth no one of them is
simply subordinated to another; each is an equally necessary factor in the being and development of the whole.

Moreover, in the purely historical sense there is no absolute "first" or "second," no strictly "earlier" or "later." History, viewed as spiritual, is in no sense a mere succession of
events separating and supplanting each other in time. It
is, in the midst of this change, an eternal present—a ὁμοῦ
πᾶν. Its "meaning" is in no one of its moments; and yet, in
each of them it is complete and unbroken.

But here the historical "problem of origin," which had
played so important a role in Herder's first studies, particularly in his prize essay on the origin of language, is transformed and raised to a higher plane of observation. The
historical *point of vision* is never abandoned; but it becomes apparent that the historical horizon itself cannot be
seen in its full scope and freedom, unless the historical
problem is united with a systematic one. What is required
now is no mere genetic account, but a "phenomenology of
spirit." But Herder does not understand phenomenology
in the sense in which Hegel understood it. For him there is
no fixed course, predetermined and necessitated by the
nature of spirit, which leads with immanent necessity from
one form of appearance to another in a uniform rhythm,
in the three stages of the dialectic, until at last after running
through all forms the end returns again to the beginning.

Herder makes no such attempt to capture the ever-flowing life of history within the orbit of metaphysical thought. Instead, for him another problem emerges, which, to be sure, is only visible in his work in an initial and still undefined outline.

As he continues to penetrate more deeply into the peculiar "nature" of language, into the nature of poetry, into the world of myth and that of history, the question as to our knowledge of reality assumes an ever more complex form and undergoes an ever richer articulation. Now it becomes clear and unmistakable that this question is not only unsolved, but cannot even be stated in its true and full sense, so long as "physical" objects constitute the only theme and goal of inquiry. The physical cosmos, the universe of natural science, constitutes only an example and paradigm for a much more general inquiry. It is this inquiry which now gradually supplants that ideal of the pan-mathematic, the *mathesis universalis,* which had dominated philosophical thought since Descartes. It is not only in the mathematical and physico-astronomical world that the *idea* of a cosmos, the idea of a thoroughgoing order, presents itself. This idea is not limited to the lawfulness of the phenomena of nature, to the world of "matter." We encounter it wherever a determinate and unified lawful structure becomes apparent within multiplicity and diversity. The "holding good" of such a lawful structure—this, in the fullest sense of the term, is the most general manifestation of what we mean by "objectivity."

In order to arrive at full clarity on this point, we need only remind ourselves of the fundamental concept of "cosmos" which ancient thought had firmly established. A "cosmos," an objective order and determination, is present wherever individual persons relate themselves to and participate in a "common world." The construction of our conception of the physical world, with sense perception as its medium, is not the only instance of such a cosmos. The possibility and necessity of such a "breaking free" of the limitations of individuality emerges nowhere so clearly and indubitably as in the phenomenon of speech. The spoken *word* never originates in the mere sound or utterance. For a word is an intended meaning. It is construed within the organic whole of a "communication," and communication "exists" only when the word passes from one person to another fusing both into one living dialogue. Thus, understanding through linguistic communication becomes for Herder, as it had been for Heraclitus, the genuine and typical expression of our understanding of the world. *Logos* creates the bond between the individual and the whole; it gives assurance to the individual that, instead of being enclosed within the waywardness of his own ego, the ἰδίη φρόνησις, he is capable of a universal existence, one κοινον καὶ θεῖον.

From the rationality invested in language and expressed in its concepts the path points to the rationality of science. For, with the resources peculiarly its own, language is not able to generate scientific knowledge, or even to arrive at it. Nevertheless, it is an indispensable stage on the way to it; it constitutes the only medium in which the knowledge of things can arise and progressively develop. The act of naming is the indispensable first step and condition of that act of determination which constitutes the task peculiar to pure science. There follows from this both the fact that, and the reason why, the theory of language constitutes a necessary and component factor in the development of epistemology.

Whoever begins the critique of knowledge with the theory of science—with the analysis of the fundamental concepts and principles of mathematics, physics, biology, or history—is, so to speak, applying leverage at too high a point. But those, too, are mistaken for whom knowledge is nothing more than a simple corroboration of what is, of what is immediately given to us in elements of sense perception. Moreover, insofar as it is not influenced by epistemological presuppositions, psychological analysis enables this fact to stand out clearly. For it shows us that language is never a simple copy of contents and relations, which sensation presents to us immediately. Its ideas are by no means the mere copies of impressions demanded by the dogma of sensationalism. On the contrary, language is a determinate and fundamental tendency of the mind's activity—an ensemble of psychological and intellectual acts; and it is in these acts that a new aspect of reality—the actuality of things—first discloses itself to us.

It was Wilhelm von Humboldt, a student of both Herder and Kant, who gave coinage to the statement that the language function cannot be an affect. It is not a mere result but a continuous self-renewing process; and the contour of man's "world" defines itself more clearly and determinately in direct proportion to the development of this process. Thus a name is not simply tacked on to its completed and ready-to-be-used objective intuition as an *extraneous symbolizing* of knowledge; instead, in it there is expressed a determinate way, a manner, and tendency for *coming to know*.

Everything we know concerning the development of language in children gives factual substantiation to this basic view. For it is manifestly not the case that in this development a fixed stage of already acquired objective intuition is strung on to a subsequent stage, in which this new acquisition is now also named, defined, and grasped by words. Quite the contrary, language awareness—the awakening symbol consciousness—impresses *its* stamp upon observation and perception in ever increasing measure as it grows in strength and extends and clarifies itself. Both observation and perception become "objective" just to the degree that this linguistic energy succeeds in clarifying, differentiating, and organizing the mute, undifferentiated chaos of particular circumstances. Linguistic symbolism opens up an original phase of spiritual and intellectual life. A life of "meanings" supplants the life of mere impulses, and of absorption into the immediate impression and the urgency of the moment. These meanings constitute something repeatable and recurring, something which is not limited to the bare here-and-now but which comes to be meant and understood as one-and-the-same in countless life-moments and in the appropriation and use of countless other persons.

By virtue of this identity of meaning—transcending the multiplicity and diversity of momentary impressions—there emerges, gradually and by stages, a determinate "stability," a "common cosmos." What we call "learning" a language is, accordingly, never a purely receptive or reproductive process, but one that is productive in the highest degree. In this process the ego not only gains insight into an enduring order but shares in constructing it. For the ego does not win its share in this order by simply joining itself to it, as to something present and given; instead, it gains its share in it [only through the process by which, and] *as* each particular, each individual, acquires order, and it contributes to the maintenance and renewal of this order in and by virtue of this [process of] acquisition.

Hence we may say from a genetic point of view that language is the first "common world" which the individual enters and that it is through the mediation of language that the intuition of an objective reality is first disclosed to him. Even in relatively advanced phases of this development it is evident again and again how closely and indissolubly they are interlaced and bound together. For the adult in learning a new language likewise does not merely acquire an increase of new sounds or signs. As soon as he enters into the "spirit" of the language, as soon as he begins to think and live in it, a new sphere of objective intuition also discloses itself to him. Intuition has not only gained in breadth but also in clarity and determinateness. At this moment, the new symbol-world begins to group, to articulate, and to organize the contents of experience and intuition in new ways.[6]

Only on the basis of such considerations can we bring to full clarity the difference between the problem of objectivity for philosophy and for the particular sciences. Aristotle was the first to reduce this difference to a precise formula. He states that philosophy is the study of being in general, that it treats of "beings as beings." The individual sciences always contemplate a particular kind of object and seek its constitution and determination; metaphysics, πρώτη φιλοσοφία, is concerned with existence as such, with ὂν ᾗ ὄν.

6. I have made only a brief attempt here to indicate the actual circumstances; for further substantiation I must refer the reader to the thorough statement of the problem which I have given in my essay, "Le language et la construction du monde des objets," *Journal de Psychologie Normale et Pathologique*, XXX (1933), 18–44.
[Originally published in German in *Bericht über den XII. Kongress der deutschen Gesellschaft für Psychologie. Hamburg* (Jena: G. Fischer, 1932) and reprinted in French in *Psychologie du Language*, by H. Delacroix, E. Cassirer, et al, *Bibliothèque de Philosophie contemporaine* (Paris: Alcan, 1933), pp. 18–44.]

But this distinction of kinds and goals of knowledge *leads* with Aristotle, and with all who have followed him, to a distinction within objectivity itself. The logical distinction corresponds to an ontological distinction. By virtue of the form of this knowledge, what is known philosophically is removed above the sphere of empirical apprehension. In contrast to the empirically conditioned, it becomes an unconditioned, a being in itself, an absolute.

Kant's critical philosophy has brought an end to this absolutism in metaphysics. But, at the same time, this end was a new beginning. For this critique also endeavors to differentiate itself from the empiricism and positivism of the particular sciences; it, too, strives for a universal grasp, for a universal solution, of the problem of "objectivity." Kant was able to carry out this solution only through inquiry into the particular sciences themselves, and by adhering strictly to their organization. He begins with pure mathematics in order to advance to the mathematical science of nature; and, again, in the *Critique of Judgment* he widens the sphere of inquiry as he probes for the fundamental concepts which make knowledge of living phenomena possible. But he has not endeavored to give a structural analysis of the "humanities" [*"Kulturwissenschaften"*] in the same sense in which he has for the natural sciences.

But this by no means points to an immanent and necessary limit to the task of critical philosophy. It indicates rather a merely historical, and to this degree, accidental limit, which resulted from the state of knowledge in the eighteenth century. With the falling away of this limitation, with the emergence, since Romanticism, of an independent science of linguistics, a science of art, and a science of religion, the general theory of knowledge found itself faced with new problems.

At the same time, it is clear from the present shape of the particular sciences that we can no longer make the same separation between philosophy and the individual sciences that was attempted by the empirical and positivistic systems of the nineteenth century. We can no longer relegate the particular sciences to the acquisition and grouping of "facts," while reserving the study of "principles" to philosophy. This separation between the "factual" and the "theoretical" is thoroughly artificial; it cuts to pieces the organic nature of thought. There are no "naked" facts other than those which can be fixed by reference to, and with the aid of, determinate presuppositions. Every substantiation of fact is possible only within a determinate judgment-entailing relationship [*Urteils-Zusammenhang*], which in turn rests on certain logical conditions.

Accordingly, "appearances" and "values" are not two spheres which admit, as it were, of being spacially removed from one another, and between which there runs a fixed boundary. Rather, they are factors correlative to each other, first producing within this correlativity the basic and original fixity of knowledge. In this regard it is scientific experimentation itself which constitutes the decisive repudiation of certain doctrines of dogmatic *empiricism*. Even in the sphere of exact science it is evident that "empirical method" and "theory"—knowledge of fact and knowledge of principle—are correlative. In the development of science, the Heraclitean saying, that the way up and the way down are the same, holds good: ὁδὸς ἄνω κάτω μίη. The more the structure of science develops, and the more sophisticated it becomes, the more it requires proof, and continual renewal, of its basis. It belongs to the very essence of every science, according to Hilbert, that a "lowering of the foundations" must accompany the influx of new facts. If this is true, it is also clear that, and why, the work of discovering and establishing the principles of the separate sciences cannot be deduced, or borrowed, from a particular philosophical discipline, from "epistemology" or methodology.

But what inquiry and what claim remain for philosophy if even this domain of questions is more and more claimed by the separate sciences? Are we not forced finally to relinquish the old dream of metaphysics and the old claim by philosophy of positing "a being qua being," to allow each separate science, instead, to carry out *its* understanding of being and to define *its* subject matter in *its* own manner and with *its* own means?

If, however, the time has come when philosophy itself must decide on a new interpretation of its own concept, it still finds itself confronted with the enigmatic problem of "objectivity," the burden of which cannot be entirely assumed by the separate sciences. For, taken in its full generality, this problem belongs to a sphere which cannot be comprehended and exhausted by science taken as a whole. Science is only one member and one factor in the system of "symbolic forms." In a certain sense it can be regarded as the keystone in the edifice of these forms; but it does not stand alone and it cannot perform its specific function without the coexistence of other energies, sharing with it in the task of "synoptic vision," of spiritual "synthesis."

The statement, that concepts without percepts are empty, also holds good here. The concept seeks to encompass the whole of the phenomena; and it reaches its goal by way of classification, subsumption, and subordination. It arranges the manifold into ways and kinds, and it defines it according to universal rules, which in themselves constitute a tightly unified system in which each single phenomenon and each particular law is assigned to its place. But in this the logical order must be tied throughout to a perceptual order. It is by no means the case that "logic" or conceptual and scientific knowledge perfects itself in a vacuum. It encounters no absolutely amorphous stuff on which to exercise its formative power. Even the "matter" of logic, those particulars which it presupposes in order to raise them to universality, is not absolutely structureless. The structureless could not only not be thought, it could not even become objectively seen, or an object of awareness.

The world of language and the world of art immediately afford us evidence of this pre-logical structuring, of this "stamped form," which antecedently lies at the basis of logical concepts. They show us ways of ordering which move along other paths and obey other laws than logical subordination of concepts. We have already made this clear in the case of language; but it holds equally for the organic nature of the arts. Sculpture, painting, and architecture are obliged to divide up a common subject matter. What comes to presentation in the arts appears to be the all-encompassing "pure intuition" of space. Still, the space of the painter, the sculptor, and the architect are not "the same." For in each of them there is expressed a specific and unique manner of apprehension, of spacial "vision."[7] All of these manifold "perspectives" serve, on the one hand, to distinguish the arts from each other and, on the other hand, they mutually illuminate one another, and hence serve to unite the arts from a higher point of view.

This separation and reintegration, διάκρισις and σύγκρισις, is what Plato envisaged as the task of "dialectic," the truly basic philosophical science. Supported by Platonic dialectic, ancient thought constructed a metaphysical picture of

7. Cf. esp. Adolf Hildebrandt, *The Problem of Form in Painting and Sculpture* (New York: G. E. Steckert & Co., 1907).

the world which has dominated and characterized all intellectual development for two millennia. The "intellectual revolution" which began with Kant declared this vision of the world to be incapable of scientific support. But while Kant thus denied the claims of any metaphysical doctrine of being, in doing so he by no means meant to give up the unity and universality of "reason." It was not intended that this should be undermined by his critique; instead, it was to be assured and established upon a new basis. Here the task of philosophy is no longer that of understanding a universal being, as against particular beings accessible only to the separate sciences, or of establishing an *ontologia generalis,* a knowledge of the transcendent, as against empirical knowledge. This form of knowledge, knowledge of ὄν ᾗ ὄν, and the hypothesis of an *absolute* object is renounced. For Kant "cognition by reason" is distinguished still more strictly and clearly from mere "cognition by the understanding." But instead of seeking an object in itself beyond these latter, an object free of the cognitive conditions of the understanding, reason seeks the "unconditioned" *within* the systematic totality of conditions themselves. In place of the unity of objects, we have here a *unity of function.* In order to achieve its goal there is no longer any need for philosophy to vie with the particular sciences within the spheres proper to them. She can allow them their full autonomy—their freedom and their self-legislation. For philosophy does not seek to limit or suppress any of these particular laws. She seeks, instead, to comprehend their totality within a systematic unity and to understand it as such. In place of a "thing in itself," an object "beyond" and "behind" the world of appearances, it seeks the manifold, the fullness and inner diversity of "appearances themselves."

This fullness is comprehensible to the human mind only

by virture of the fact that it possesses the power of differentiating itself within itself. For each new problem that it encounters it constructs a new form of understanding. In *this*
respect a "philosophy of symbolic forms" can make good the
claim of unity and universality, which metaphysics in its
dogmatic form must abandon. Not only can it unite these
various modes and directions of our knowledge of the
world; over and above this, it is capable of evaluating every
attempt at understanding the world, every analysis of it
which the human mind is capable of, and of conceiving each
in its true character. It is in this manner that the problem of
objectivity first becomes visible in its full scope; and taken
in this sense it encompasses not only the cosmos of nature
but also that of culture.[8]

2

After countless and continually renewed attempts, and
after unending quarrels between schools of philosophy,
nineteenth-century science appears finally to have assigned
the problem of "philosophical anthropology" to its proper
place. The question, "What is man?" has led repeatedly to
insoluble problems whenever—in conformity with the basic
doctrines of Platonism, Christianity, and Kantian philosophy—man has been made into a "citizen of two worlds."
Only in the science of the nineteenth century is this boundary removed. It is able to establish man's proper status
without having to set him over against and above nature.
The term "evolution" was declared to be the key to all previous riddles of nature and all "riddles of the universe."

8. The interpretation of the nature and task of philosophy pre-
sented here is more thoroughly presented and substantiated in the
Introduction to my *Philosophy of Symbolic Forms* (New Haven: Yale
University Press, 1953) Vol. I.

Seen from this standpoint, the antithesis between "culture" and "nature" loses all dialectical sharpness. This antithesis was lost as soon as the problem was successfully removed from a metaphysical basis to a biological basis and approached and handled within a purely biological perspective.

To be sure, the concept of evolution cannot be claimed as an achievement of modern science. It goes back to the first beginnings of Greek philosophy. Indeed, at the highpoint of this philosophy, it looms as one of the most convincing means with which to break the sway of Platonic "dualism." This task is set forth with full consciousness by Aristotle. But in its Aristotelian form the concept of evolution is not yet equal to this task. For it miscarries just before the last decisive question on which it must prove itself. Aristotle depicts organic nature and the series of living beings as an ascending development leading from one form to the next. Even the human soul, in the broad sense—understood merely as "vegetative" or "sensitive" soul—is, for him, nothing but a natural form, bound as such to a specific body. It is the "entelechy" of an organic body.

Still, the Aristotelian psychology *as a whole* does not admit of being reduced to biology. For a residue remains which cannot be completely expunged by Aristotle himself nor by any of his students and followers. The "thinking" soul defies all attempts to reduce it to the elementary functions of the nutritive or sensitive soul. It has affirmed its own and exceptional position; accordingly, it must eventually be assigned another and independent origin. If, in the Aristotelian psychology, we proceed from perception to memory, from this to representation (φαντασία), and from here to conceptual thought, the principle of ascending development maintains itself at each of these stages. But then we suddenly find ourselves led to a point from which a leap is unavoidable. For the "power of thought" in its highest and purest manifestation cannot be reached in this manner. It is and remains a *function which is an end in itself*. The "active intellect" belongs to the spiritual world, without the possibility of its being explained in terms of the elements of organic life. Thus, here again the dualism breaks forth. It receives its unambiguous expression when Aristotle declares that νοῦς, the power of thought, has fallen here from outside (θύραθεν) the world of living things.

The fact that Aristotelian metaphysics and psychology were not able to close these gaps is understandable. For the Aristotelian concept of form is rooted in the Platonic conception of ideas and it remains bound to it in essential presuppositions, even when it seems farthest removed. The modern theory of evolution is the first to be determined to draw the final consequence. It takes the requirement of continuity seriously and extends it to all domains. Just as the higher forms of life are bound to the more elementary forms by smooth transitions, so likewise, they can exhibit no functions which forsake the dimension of organic existence as such. Whatever towers above this place and seems to belong to "another world" is and remains a mere castle in the air, inasmuch as it is not possible to show how it emerged from a fundamental and elementary level of life and continues to depend upon it. Here a truly biological vision of the world must come into its own. What the speculative concept of evolution failed to accomplish—whether that of Aristotle, Leibniz, or Hegel—must and will be accomplished by the empirical concept of evolution. Only with it is the way to a strictly "monistic" interpretation opened up; only now is the cleft between "nature" and "spirit" closed. Viewed in this perspective, the Darwinian theory claims not only to contain the answer to the problem of the origin of man but also the answer to all the questions as to the origin of human culture. When Darwin's theory first appeared, it seemed finally, after centuries of vain efforts, to have revealed the uniting bond that encompasses natural science and the humanities.

In the year 1863, August Schleicher published his work, *Die Darwinsche Theorie und die Sprachwissenschaft* [Linguistics and the Darwinian Theory].[9] The mere program of a science of civilization on Darwinian principles is fully defined here. Schleicher himself began initially on the basis of Hegel's doctrine. Later he became convinced that the solution could not lie there. He demanded, on principle, a reconstruction of the method of linguistics which would, for the first time, elevate it to [a form of knowledge] having the same validity as natural science.[10] Here, finally, a foundation appeared to have been laid which was common to physics, biology, and linguistics—and hence to all the self-styled *"Geisteswissenschaften"* [moral sciences]. One and the same causality would embrace all three fields of study and extinguish all ultimate distinctions between them.

The first reaction against this conception began in the last decade of the nineteenth century, just as doubt concerning the validity of the Darwinian theory became ever more pronounced in biology itself. Attention now became focused not only upon the empirical limits of the theory, but

9. [August Schleicher, *Darwinism Tested by the Science of Language*, trans. A.V.W. Bikkers, with preface and additional notes (London, 1869).

N.B. The text gives 1873 as the first publication date for the above work by Schleicher. But this is clearly an error.]

10. For further details concerning Schleicher's theory see my *Philosophy of Symbolic Forms*, I, 164 ff.

also, and in far stronger measure than heretofore, upon the certainty of its philosophical foundations. Here, unexpectedly, the concept of form experiences a new resurrection. Vitalism immediately latches on to this concept, and with this support it attempts to carry through its thesis of the "autonomy of the organic" and the autonomy of living beings. We shall follow this movement only insofar as it has influenced the problem of establishing the basic principles of the humanities and their logical validity. This problem, as such, was foreign to the true champions of vitalism. Even as metaphysician, Driesch was a philosopher of nature. At no time did he attempt to construct a logic of the humanities. Indeed, he would be obliged on the basis of his systematic presuppositions to doubt the possibility of such a logic. He vigorously contested the scientific validity of history. Nevertheless, this new orientation in thinking introduced by vitalism also influenced our problem—though only indirectly, to be sure. It is instructive to pursue this influence; for in effective ways it contributed to this later work and in many respects cleared the ground for it, although its true and essential impulse was in support of wholly other motives and concerns.

Uexküll once stated that the materialism of the nineteenth century, in teaching that all reality subsists and exhausts itself within matter and force, has completely overlooked a third essential factor. It had blinded itself to *form,* which alone is decisive and determining.[11] Uexküll is determined to restore this factor to its rightful position in his *Theoretical Biology;* but, on the other hand, he is determined to keep it free of all metaphysical and psychological border-concepts. He speaks solely as an anatomist, as an ob-

11. Jacob Uexküll, *Die Lebenslehre* (Potsdam: Müller & Kiepenheuer Verlag, 1930), p. 19.

jective natural scientist. According to him, the study of
anatomy is capable of furnishing strict proof that every organism presents a self-enclosed world in which every con-
stituent "weaves itself into the whole." The organism is no
aggregate of parts, but a system of functions which condition each other. In the "blueprint" of every animal we
would be able to read off immediately the nature of this
interaction. "The theory of the living being," according to
Uexküll, "is a pure natural science and has only one goal—
the search for the blueprints of living beings, their origin
and their function." Nor can the essence of any organism be
conceived as self-sufficient, in isolation from its "environment." What constitutes its specific nature is its peculiar
relationship to this environment—the manner in which it
receives its stimuli and modifies them within itself.

Study of these blueprints shows that, in this respect, there
is no difference between the lower forms of life and the most
highly developed. For each ever-so-elementary organism we
can establish a determinate "stimulus pattern" and a determinate "effector pattern" and in each we can explain how
its various "functional circuits" interact with each other.
According to Uexküll, this *interaction is* the manifestation
and the basal phenomenon of life as such. Those stimuli
from the external world which the animal is able to receive,
by virtue of its basic structure, constitute the only reality
present for it, and, because of this physical limit, all other
spheres of existence are closed to it.[12]

This task for modern biology, which is set forth with
great originality and carried out with extraordinary fruit-

12. Jakob von Uexküll, *Theoretical Biology,* trans. D. L. MacKin-
non (New York: Harcourt, 1926). Cf. completely revised 2d ed., *Theoretische Biologie* (Berlin: J. Springer, 1928). Cf. also *Die Lebenslehre*
(Potsdam: Müller & Kiepenheuer, 1930).

fulness in Uexküll's writings, also affords us a path that can lead to a clear and definite delineation of the boundary between "life" and "spirit," between the world of organic forms and the world of cultural forms. Time and again the attempt has been made to describe this distinction as if it were physical. We have sought for external features by which to characterize man, and by which he was supposed to be elevated above other life forms. It is well known what fanciful constructions have been tied, again and again, to such features, for example, to the upright gait of the human being. But the advance of empirical knowledge has torn down all of these separations we have sought to erect between man and organic nature. Unity of nature has triumphed here [over the earlier dualisms] with ever increasing clarity and success. In his discovery of the intermaxillary bone Goethe saw one of the most compelling and significant confirmations of the argument that no form of nature is absolutely unrelated and cut off from the others.

The distinguishing trait we are looking for is not a physical but a *functional* distinction. What is distinctive about the world of culture cannot be understood and described by pointing out specific distinguishing features. For the decisive change lies, not in the emergence of new features and properties, but in the characteristic *change of function* which all determinations undergo as soon as we pass from the animal world to the human world. Here, and here alone, is it possible to establish a real μετάβασις εἰς ἄλλο γένος. The "freedom" which man is able to wrest for himself does not imply that he has removed himself from nature, from her being and operations. He cannot overturn or break through the organic limits which are fixed for him just as for any other living being. But within these limits, indeed by means of them, he fashions a breadth and self-sufficiency of movement which is accessible and attainable only by him. Uexküll once remarked that the formal structure [*Bauplan*] of each living being, and hence the determinate relationship between its stimulus world and its functional world, encloses this being as firmly as the walls of a prison. Nor does the human being escape this prison by destroying its walls; he escapes only by becoming conscious of them. Here the Hegelian statement holds good—that he who knows about a limitation is already free of it. This becoming aware is the beginning and end, the alpha and omega, of human freedom. Knowing and taking account of necessity is the genuine process of liberation which "spirit," in contradistinction to "nature," has brought to perfection.

The various symbolic forms—myth, language, art, and science—constitute the indispensable precondition for this process. They are the true media—which man himself has created—by virtue of which he has been able to separate himself from the world, and in this very separation, to bind himself all the closer to it. This feature of mediation characterizes all human knowledge. It is also distinctive and typical of all human action.

Even plants and animals maintain themselves by means of the fact that they not only receive stimuli continually from their environment but also, in a certain manner, "answer" them. And each organism perfects this answer in a different way. Here we find the most diverse and delicate gradations, as Uexküll has shown in his *Umwelt und Innenwelt der Tiere* [The Outer World and the Inner World of Animals].[13] On the whole, however, for the animal world a fixed and unified response always follows from the same conditions. The answer must join the stimulus in immediate

13. Jakob von Uexküll, *Umwelt und Innenwelt der Tiere*, 2d ed. (Berlin: J. Springer, 1921).

temporal sequence and proceed always in the same way. What we term animal "instincts" are nothing other than such fixed chains of actions, whose single links engage each other in ways predetermined by the nature of the animal. A specific situation works as an impulse to action, which releases certain movements; to this first impulse others and still others add themselves until a determinate "melody of impulses" runs off in the same settled manner. The animal plays this melody; but it cannot engage it at will. The path which it must traverse in order to solve a definite task opens up; the animal pursues it without having to seek for it and without being able to alter it in any significant way.

All this is fundamentally altered the moment we enter the sphere of human actions. In its simplest and most elementary forms this is characterized by an "indirectness" which is sharply opposed to the manner in which animals respond. This change in mode of behavior presents itself most clearly when man makes the transition to the use of tools. For in order to invent a tool, as such, it is necessary that man lift his gaze above the sphere of immediate needs. While fashioning them he is not acting from the impulse and necessity of the moment. Instead of being moved immediately by an actual stimulus, he looks to possible needs, to the satisfaction of which he prepares the means in advance. The purpose which the tool serves involves within itself a definite pre-vision. The impulse does not derive solely from the force of the present; instead, it belongs also to the future, which must be anticipated in some fashion in order to become effective in this way. This "pre-presentation" of the future characterizes all human action. We must set before ourselves in "images" something not yet an existing thing, in order, then, to proceed from this "possibility" to the "reality," from potency to act.

This basic feature emerges still more clearly when we turn from the practical to the theoretical sphere. For in this respect there exists no fundamental difference between the two. All theoretical concepts bear within themselves the character of "instruments." In the final analysis they are nothing other than tools, which we have fashioned for the solution of specific tasks and which must be continually re-fashioned. Concepts do not refer, like sense perceptions, to any particular "given," to a concrete and present situation; they move, rather, in the sphere of the possible and seek, as it were, to delineate the frame of the possible. The more the horizon of human representations, meanings, thoughts, and judgments is extended, the more complex becomes the system of mediators necessary to survey it. The symbols of speech are the first and most important link in this chain. But implicit within them are forms different in kind and development. One and the same *basic function,* the function of symbolism as such, unfolds itself within these divergent cardinal directions and creates ever new structures within them. It is the totality of these constructions which distinguishes and characterizes the human world. The "stimulus world" and "response world" of animals acquire something new in the human sphere—the "image world" [*"Bildwelt"*]; and it is this very world which [in turn] gains an ever increasing control over man as it develops.

Here a most difficult question arises—one with which man has had to struggle again and again in the course of the development of civilization. Have we been led into a fatal mistake by venturing on this course [into the new world of symbols]? Is it *possible* that by so doing man has torn himself loose from nature and estranged himself from the reality and immediacy of natural existence? Are the things he has exchanged for these really good? Or are they not the gravest threats to his life? If philosophy remains mindful of its proper and highest task, if it is determined to be not only a definite kind of *knowledge* but also the *conscience* of human culture, then, again and again, in the course of its history, it must be led back to this problem. Instead of giving way to a naive belief in progress, it must not only ask itself whether this envisaged "progress" is attainable but whether it is worth striving for. And once doubt on this issue has been awakened, it seems that it will not be quieted. This shows itself most forcefully when we fix our attention upon man's practical relationship to reality.

Through the use of tools man has made himself supreme over things. But, instead of a state of abundance, this supremacy itself has become a curse. The technical science which man has invented in order to control the physical world has, in fact, turned against him. It has led, not only to an ever increasing self-estrangement, but ultimately to a species of self-extinction. The tool, which appeared to be destined for the fulfillment of human needs, on the contrary, has created countless artificial needs. Each elaboration of technology is, and remains, a treacherous gift. Hence, the yearning for primitive, unbroken, immediate existence repeatedly breaks forth. The more numerous the areas of life taken over by technology, the louder the call, "Back to nature!"

Uexküll once remarked with respect to the lower animals that they are so completely adapted to their environment that each rests as peacefully and serenely in this environment as an infant in its crib. But this undisturbed serenity comes to an end as soon as we enter the human sphere.

Each animal species is firmly bound, as it were, to the circuit of its needs and drives; it has no other world than that which is defined for it by its instincts. And within this world, to which the animal is adapted by nature, there is no hesitation and no failure: the limits of its instincts immediately afford it the greatest of security.

No human knowledge and no human action can ever find its way back to such certainty and such undoubting existence. Indeed, the value of the intellectual tools man has created is even more questionable than that of his technical tools. Time and again *language* has been extravagantly praised; we have seen in it the true expression and unmistakable proof of that "reason" which elevates man above the [merely] animal. But are all the arguments which have been advanced in its behalf genuine arguments? Or are they only an empty idolatry in which language flatters itself? Are they more than rhetorical? Do they have *philosophical* merit?

In the history of philosophy there have never failed to be important philosophers who have not only warned against this identification of "language" and "reason," but have regarded language as the true adversary of "reason." To them it is not the guide but the perpetual seducer of human knowledge. They insist that cognition will only reach its goal when it resolutely turns its back on language and no longer allows itself to be deceived as to her nature. "In vain do we extend our view into the heavens and pry into the entrails of the earth," says Berkeley, "in vain do we consult the writings of learned men and trace the dark footsteps of antiquity; we need only draw the curtain of words to behold the fairest tree of knowledge, whose fruit is excellent, and within the reach of our hands."[14]

Berkeley himself has not been able to find his way out of this conflict except by freeing philosophy not only from

14. Concerning Berkeley's criticism of language, see my *Philosophy of Symbolic Forms*, I, 136 ff.

the domination of language but also from that of "concepts." For, to Berkeley, the conclusion is inescapable, that concepts, being universal and abstract, are not only related to that universality manifest in names and words but are inseparable from them. Hence, only a radical solution will help matters: reality must also be denied to concepts, to "logic," and must be limited to pure observation, to the sphere of "perception." Wherever we leave this sphere, wherever we proceed from *percipi* to *concipi*, there again, we find ourselves under the tyranny of words. All logical cognition completes itself in acts of judgment, in theoretical reflection. But the very term "reflection" signifies the poverty which adheres to it unavoidably. The "reflected" object is never the object itself. Indeed, each new mirroring surface we turn to threatens to remove us further and further from the original and from the initial truth.

Since ancient times such considerations have constituted the breeding ground of theoretical skepticism. In the course of its history the theory of art, as well as the theory of language has had to struggle continuously with similar problems. Plato forsook and condemned art. He condemned it because in the struggle between truth and appearance it stood, not on the side of philosophy but on the side of sophistry. The artist does not contemplate the ideas, the eternal paradigms of truth; instead, he wanders around in the realm of copies and turns all his energy to shaping copies which fake the reality of that which they imitate. The poet and the painter are like the sophist—the perpetual "image maker (εἰδωλοποιός). Instead of conceiving being as what it is, both deceive us with illusions of being. So long as aesthetics is based on the "theory of imitation," it is vain to attempt to effectively refute this Platonic objection.

In justifying the imitation theory critics have sought not

a theoretical or aesthetic but a hedonistic justification. Aesthetic rationalism has also frequently gone in this direction. It has insisted that imitation obviously cannot exhaust its model, that the "appearance" cannot attain reality. Instead, it points to the pleasure inherent in imitation which increases the closer it approaches the model. The very first lines of Boileau's *Art Poétique* exhibit this train of thought in classical terseness and clarity. Even a monstrosity, declares Boileau, can give pleasure in an artistic presentation; for pleasure concerns not the object but the excellence of the imitation. With this there emerged at least the possibility of determining the true scope of aesthetics as such and of granting it an independent value, even though this goal could only be reached by way of a curious detour.

But a definitive solution of the problem was not to be had on the basis of strict rationalism and metaphysical dogmatism. For if we are convinced that the logical concept is the necessary and sufficient condition for cognition of the essence of things, all else that is specifically different and that does not meet this standard of clarity and distinctness is only unreal appearance. In this case the illusion-character of those intellectual forms which remain outside the sphere of the purely logical is indisputable. It can only be exhibited as such, and explained and justified, to the extent that we investigate the psychological origin of the illusion and attempt to set forth its empirical conditions in the structure of human representation and phantasy.

The problem takes on a completely different shape if, instead of treating objects as firmly fixed in the beginning, we view them, so to speak, from an infinitely distant point, toward which all knowing and understanding aim. In this case, the "given" of objects becomes the "problem" of objectivity. And clearly it is not *only* theoretical knowledge which participates in this *task;* on the contrary, every energy of the mind shares in it. Language and art also are able to exhibit their particular "objective" meanings—not because they imitate a self-subsisting reality, but because they anticipate [*vor-bilden*] it, because they constitute distinct directions and modes of objectification. And this holds for the world of inner experience, just as it holds for the world of outer experience.

For metaphysics and the doctrine of dualism, "soul" and "body," "inner" and "outer" signify two spheres of being strictly cut off from each other. They are able to influence each other, even though this influence becomes ever more mysterious and problematic the more metaphysics draws its own consequences. But the radical distinction between them is not to be overcome. Here "subjectivity" and "objectivity" will always constitute spheres unto themselves, and the analysis of a distinct form of spiritual energy could then appear to be successful and complete only if we arrived at clarity as to which sphere it belongs to. Thus a species of either-or would obtain—a "this side" or a "that side"—the decision being conceived as a kind of spacial definition, which refers any phenomenon to its place in consciousness or in being, the inner world or the outer world.

For the critical interpretation even this *alternative* dissolves into a dialectical illusion. For our interpretation seeks to show that the inner and outer experience are not two foreign and separated things, but that they subsist by virtue of common conditions, and that they can come to be only in conjunction and in continuous interrelation. Instead of *separation of substances,* there is *correlativity of relationship* and *of fulfillment.*

It is by no means the case that this reciprocal relationship holds only for scientific knowledge. It obtains also when we look beyond the sphere of knowledge and theoretical concepts. No simple opposition of "I" and "world" determines matters in language, nor in art, nor indeed even in myth and religion. Here, too, the intuition of both [ego and world] is built up within one and the same process, [a process] which leads to a continual "setting apart" of the two poles. This process could be *reduced* by analysis in the proper sense only if the reciprocal relationship could be overcome, if it were possible for it to lead to an isolation of the subject and object poles. Here, too, the bifurcation— symbol or object—shows itself to be impossible; indeed, more careful analysis shows us that it is the *function* of symbolism itself which constitutes the precondition for all grasp of "objects" or factual relationships. With this insight the contrast between appearance and reality assumes a different character and a different significance.

In the case of art it becomes immediately evident that to renounce "appearance" categorically is to abandon also the "phenomenon" and the object of artistic intuition and construction. For it is in the "colorful splendor" and in it alone that the painting has its fitting and genuine existence. No artist can present nature without revealing himself in and through this presentation. And no artistic expression of the self is possible except that something material be set before us in all its plasticity and objectivity. A great work of art only comes into being when the subjective and the objective, feeling and form, pass completely into each other and when each derives its being entirely from the other. From this it is evident that, and why, the work of art can never be a mere copying of either the subjective or the objective, the spiritual or the material world, but that a genuine discovery of both [of these correlative factors] perfects itself in this process—a discovery which, in its universal character, is fully as significant as theoretical knowledge.

In this sense, and to the extent that we can have knowledge through visible and tangible forms, Goethe was right in saying that *style* is rooted in the deepest foundations of knowledge, in the very being of things. Indeed, if art could do no more than simply repeat an external fact or an inner event, it would remain a most dubious, or in any case, a pitiable achievement. If art were a copy of existence in this sense, all of Plato's objections to it would be justified: we would be forced to deny it any measure of "ideal" significance. For true ideality—that of intuitive formation as well as that of theoretical concepts—always entails a productive rather than a merely receptive or imitative relation [of subject and object]. It discovers something new instead of repeating something old under a different form. Art remains an idle amusement of the mind, an empty play, when it is not directed to this basic task.

To merely glance at a truly great work of art is to become conscious of this basic character. Always it leaves us with the impression that we have encountered something new, something we had not known before. It is no mere imitation or repetition that stands before us. Here the world always seems to be revealed for us in new ways and from new angles. If the epic could do no more than fix past events and renew them in men's memories, there would be nothing to distinguish it from mere chronicle. But we need only to think of Homer, Dante, and Milton to be convinced that in every great epic of world literature it is something quite different that faces us. Here we are not confronted with a mere report of something past; instead, we are translated by the threads of the epic tale into a world-perspective in which we are now able to see the totality of events and the entire world of man in a new light. This quality is characteristic even of patently "subjective" art, even of the *lyric*. The lyric, more than any other species of art, seems imprisoned by the moment. The lyric poem seeks to seize in flight and hold fast a unique, fleeting, never-to-recur state of awareness. It springs into being in a single moment and does not look beyond this moment. Yet even in lyric poetry, and perhaps in it above all, there is to be seen that species of "ideality" which Goethe has characterized as the original, the ideal mode of thought, the eternal within the ephemeral. By losing itself in the moment, seeking nothing else than to exhaust it of its entire mood and atmosphere, it thereby invests it with duration and eternity.

If the lyric poem were to do nothing else than to fix in words the momentary and individual feelings of poets, it would not be different from any other verbal expression. All lyricism would be merely verbal expression, all speech would be lyricism. Benedetto Croce has in fact drawn this conclusion in his aesthetic. But in addition to the *genus proximum* of expression we must fix our attention everywhere upon the specific difference of lyric expression. The lyric is no mere intensification or sublimation of an exclamation. It is no mere divulging of a momentary mood nor does it seek simply to traverse the scale of tones between extremes of emotion, between sorrow and joy, pain and pleasure, serenity and despair. If the lyric poet succeeds in giving "melody and voice" to pain, by so doing, he has not only enveloped it in a new covering; he has changed its inner nature. Through the medium of the emotions he has enabled us to glimpse spiritual depths which until now were closed and inaccessible to himself as well as to us.

But we need only remind ourselves of the genuine highpoints and turning points in the development of lyric style to become convinced of this basic character. While he seeks merely to express himself, every great lyricist gives us knowledge of a new feeling for the world. He shows us life and reality in a form in which we feel we have never known it before. A song by Sappho, an ode by Pindar, Dante's *Vita nuova*, Petrarch's sonnets, Goethe's *Sesenheimer Lieder* and *West-östlicher Divan*, Hölderlin's or Leopardi's poems— these give us more than a series of flitting emotions, which unfold before us only to vanish again and lose themselves in nothingness. All this "is" and "endures"; it discloses to us a *knowledge* which cannot be grasped in abstract concepts, which stands before us, nevertheless, as the revelation of something new, something never before known or familiar. As its greatest achievement, we owe to art the fact that in its particulars it allows us to feel and to know what is objective; that it places all its objective creations before us with a concreteness and individuality which floods them with a life of strength and intensity.

CHAPTER 2

Perception of Things
and Perception of Expression

THE INNER CRISIS in science and philosophy in the last hundred years, since the deaths of Goethe and Hegel, stands out in no other feature so clearly, perhaps, as in the relationship existing between natural science and the humanities. In both fields of study progress in research signified a victorious campaign without equal and without interruption. This epoch is virtually unique, not only in content, but also in method, and not only in continuous expansion of materials, but also in its intellectual development and penetration.

Exact science has not only progressively widened its sphere; it has also fashioned wholly new instruments of knowledge. Biology has advanced beyond mere description and classification of natural forms and has become a genuine theory of organic forms.

What has taken the humanities [*Kulturwissenschaften*] by surprise is, perhaps, an even greater task. For here it is first of all a question of finding that "sure road to knowledge," which even Kant believed could only be reserved for mathematics and the mathematical science of nature. Since the days of Romanticism, history, classical studies, archeology, linguistics, the critical study of literature and art, comparative mythology, and the comparative study of religion have continually made contributions in this direction. They have conceived their task ever more precisely and have developed their specific instruments of thought and research with increasing finesse. But in the face of all these triumphs of knowledge, achieved within the course of a single century, there loomed a serious defect, an internal wound. Even though research was able to advance continually in each of these fields of study, the inner unity of each became ever more problematic.

Philosophy was unable to contend for this unity, nor was it able to put a stop to the growing fragmentation. Hegel's system is the last great attempt to comprehend the whole of knowledge and to organize it by virtue of one ruling idea. But Hegel was not able to reach his goal. For the balance of forces which he wished to establish proves to be a mere illusion. Hegel's concern and philosophical ambition was to reconcile "nature" and "idea." But instead of this reconciliation his result was the subordination of nature to the absolute idea. Nature retains nothing in its own right; it retains only an apparent independence. All her being she holds in fee from the idea; for she is nothing but idea itself, insofar as this latter is considered not in its absolute being and truth but in alienation from itself, in its otherness. Here is the true Achilles heel of the Hegelian system. It was unable to withstand for long the attacks which were directed against this point with increasing force.

To be sure, in themselves natural science and the arts do not appear to be affected by this fate of the Hegelian doctrine. Both are able to save their belongings from the shipwreck of the Hegelian system and they are convinced they can secure and maintain these possessions so much

the sooner the more they henceforth go their own ways,
without any philosophical guardianship. Their paths have
continued to lead in different directions; this separation
appears now to be sealed once and for all.

Instead of removing this cleft between natural science
and the humanities, the development of philosophy in the
nineteenth century served only to widen it all the more. For
now, step by step, philosophy finds itself breaking up into
the two enemy camps of naturalism and historicism. The
battle between the two becomes increasingly violent. No
mediation or reconciliation between naturalism and historicism is sanctioned; mutual understanding between them
does not seem even to be possible. In the excellent presentation of the development of historicism by Ernst Troeltsch
we are able to follow the struggle in all its various aspects.[1]
It is far less a problem in the critique of knowledge and
theory of method than an opposition of *"Weltanschauungen"* scarcely accessible to purely rational arguments.
After a brief attempt at logical clarification of this state of
affairs, the antagonists withdrew to fixed metaphysical posi-
tions, from which they could not be dislodged, but from
which, to be sure, each was able only to perpetuate itself,
without being able either to persuade or to refute the other.
Choosing between science or the humanities, between naturalism or historicism, seems to be left to the feeling and
subjective taste of the individual; more and more objective
proof gives way to polemics.

In this controversy critical philosophy has remained true
to the universal task set for it by Kant. Above all, it has
sought to restore the problem to its true basis. It sought to

1. Ernst Troeltsch, *Gesammelte Schriften von Ernst Troeltsch*
(Tübingen: Mohr, 1912–25), Bd. 3 Erstes Buch (Das logische Problem
der Geschichtsphilosophie).

remove it from the jurisdiction of metaphysics and to study it purely under the aspect of epistemology. This is the genuine achievement effected by Windelband in his speech of 1894 on "History and Natural Science." Windelband's theory does not regard the difference between natural science and history as a difference in *Weltanschauungen,* but rather as a difference in method. Hence, it cannot subscribe one-sidedly either to naturalism or to historicism. It must look upon knowledge of nature and knowledge of history as equally necessary and as equally valid factors in [any pursuit of] knowledge—factors which acquire determinateness only in their interdependence.

Windelband's distinction between "nomothetic" concepts of natural science and "idiographic" concepts of history seeks to establish this relationship. But simple and enlightening as it may appear at first, it is just in this simplicity that his distinction fails to do justice to the exceedingly complex facts which it seeks to describe. Plato required of the dialectician that he not rest content with any arbitrary conceptual distinctions. If he divides a whole according to kinds and species, he must not do violence to its structure: he must not cut, but must divide the whole in accordance with its "natural joints" (κατ' ἄρθρα ᾗ πέφυκεν). It becomes evident that Windelband's distinction does not really satisfy this requirement, especially as taken up and carried through by Rickert. He, too, makes a sharp cut between the universals of natural science and the individuals of history. But he immediately finds himself obliged to admit that, in its concrete work, science itself by no means follows the dictates of the logician—that it is forever thwarting them. Again and again, the boundaries which theory must erect are blurred by this work. Instead of clearly separate opposites, we find at most only mixed and transitional forms. Within natural science problems emerge which can only be handled by the conceptual methods of history. On the other hand, there is no reason for not applying scientific modes of inquiry to the study of historical subject matters. Every scientific concept is in fact both universal and particular: its task is to set forth the synthesis of both of these factors. Even in Rickert's theory every cognition of an historical individual entails its relation to a universal. But in place of the universal concepts of species and laws he introduces another system of reference—the system of value-concepts. To give historical order and interpretation to a fact is to relate it to universal values. Only by means of such reference does historical knowledge succeed in traversing according to fixed guiding principles the immeasurable plurality of particulars, which, as such, are inconceivable; and only by virtue of this process does it succeed in giving meaningful shape to these particulars. But at this point the theory faces a new problem whose difficulty increases the more fully we realize its real source.

Windelband and Rickert speak as disciples of Kant. They were determined to achieve for history and the humanities what Kant had achieved for the mathematical science of nature. They sought to remove both from the jurisdiction of metaphysics. Taking both as given, the conditions of their possibility were to be investigated in the manner of Kant's "transcendental" inquiry. But, if the possession of a *universal* system of values turns out to be one of these necessary conditions, the question arises as to how the historian can arrive at any such system and how its objective validity is to be established. If he seeks to establish it on the basis of history itself, he is in danger of involving himself in a circular argument. If he seeks an a priori construction of such a system, as Rickert himself has done in his

Philosophy of Value, it has been shown again and again that such a construction cannot be carried through without metaphysical assumptions, and that in the final analysis the problem ends just where it began.

Herman Paul has taken a different path from that of Windelband and Rickert in his attempt to arrive at a solution to the question as to the first principles of the humanities. He has the advantage over both of not having to remain with general conceptual distinctions, but of being able to engage in the problems directly in his own concrete research and to draw from its richness. This research assumed linguistics, and those problems which for Paul constituted the history of language, as the pattern on which he developed his fundamental views. He begins with the fact that no historical discipline can proceed in a *purely* historical manner—that a science of first principles must always accompany it. For this science Paul falls back on *psychology*.[2] With this the spell of pure historicism appears to be broken. But, on the other hand, it appears to leave linguistics and the humanities in general in immediate danger of falling prey to psychologism. Paul's own theory has not escaped this danger. In the main it is based on Herbart and constructed from his basic psychological views. But just because of this, and without being noticed, certain elements of Herbart's metaphysics make their way into the theory, jeopardizing its purely empirical character. In Karl Vossler's judgment,

> One cannot lean on the psychology of Herbart without getting his metaphysics as part of the bargain. What lies at the threshold of the empirical sciences as pure

2. Cf. Herman Paul, *Principles of the History of Language* (London: Longmans, Green and Co., 1891) pp. xxi–xxiii.

metaphysics cannot be dismissed. Actually Herbart's agnostic mysticism and his unknowable things in themselves cast a dark shadow over the whole of Paul's science of language; as a result, it is just this basic question—the question as to the nature of language—which for him is never able to emerge with clarity.[3]

But what is the meaning of this question as to the "nature" of language, or of any of the other objects of the humanities, if they are not to be taken as purely historical, purely psychological, or purely metaphysical? Is there another field of study altogether to which this question can be properly and fittingly asked? Or do these three fields completely exhaust among themselves all that pertains to the humanities?

Hegel distinguished the three spheres of subjective, objective, and absolute spirit. The phenomenology of subjective spirit studies psychology; objective spirit is present to us only in the history of spirit; and absolute spirit reveals itself to us in metaphysics. As such, this triad appears to encompass the totality of culture with all its individual forms and objects. The concept, as logical and metaphysical, does not appear to lead beyond this classification and tripartition.

Nevertheless, the distinction here at issue has still another side to it, which cannot be made fully evident by analysis of *concepts*. For here we are obliged to go back a step further. Already in *perception itself* there is to be seen a factor, which in its subsequent development leads to this very distinction. We must move our inquiry into this basic and original layer of all phenomena of consciousness in

3. Karl Vossler, *The Spirit of Language in Civilization* (London: Kegan Paul, Trench, Trubner & Co., Ltd., 1932) p. 5.

order to find in it the necessary Archimedian point, the δός μοι ποῦ στῶ. Here, in a sense, we will have dispensed with and gone beyond the limits of mere logic. Analysis of the form of concepts as such is not capable of bringing complete clarity to what specifically distinguishes the humanities from natural science. Instead we must resolve to carry the inquiry to a still deeper level. We must commit ourselves to a phenomenology of perception and ask what it can offer toward the solution of our problem.

If we attempt to describe perception in its simple phenomenal state, it appears, in a sense, to be two-faced. It contains two factors which in their inmost depths are fused, but neither of which can be reduced to the other. In meaning they remain distinct, even though it is not possible to separate them in actuality. There is no perception that does not imply a determinate "object" and that is not directed toward this object. But this necessary objective reference presents itself to us in a twofold orientation, which we may characterize briefly and schematically as orientation toward the "it" and orientation toward the "you." Always in perception there is a discernment of ego-pole and object-pole. The world which the self encounters is in the one case a thing-world and in the other a person-world. In the one case, we observe it as a completely spacial object and as the sum total of temporal transformations which complete themselves in this object; whereas, in the other case, we observe it as if it were something "like ourselves." In both cases the otherness persists; but this very fact reveals a characteristic difference. The "it" is an absolute other, an *aliud;* the "you" is an *alter ego.* There can be no mistaking the fact that, always, as we move in the one direction or the other, perception takes on a different significance for us and a distinctive coloring and tone, as it were.

That human beings experience reality in this double mode is unmistakable and indisputable. This is a matter of simple fact which no theory can throw into doubt or annihilate. Why is it so difficult for theory to admit this? Why has theory attempted again and again not only to resort to abstraction from this fact—this is thoroughly justified in point of method—but also to deny and betray it? We discover the basis for this anomaly when we become fully aware of the tendency which all theorizing derives from its origin and which increases in strength as theory advances. This tendency consists, not, to be sure, in completely suppressing, but in limiting one of these factors of perception—forever reclaiming more territory from its opposite. All theoretical explanation finds itself in opposition to another spiritual force—the force of myth. In order to protect themselves against this force, philosophy and science are obliged not only to replace particular mythical explanations but to do battle with the whole mythical interpretation of existence and to reject it *in toto*. It must not only attack the products and configurations of myth but must attack its root.

But this root is no other thing than perception of expression. Primacy of expression-perception over thing-perception is what characterizes the mythical world-view. For it, there is no fixed and separate "world of cause." For it lacks any constant unity—an attainment which is the first goal of all theoretical knowledge. Every shape can metamorphose into another; anything can come from anything. At any moment the shape of things threatens to melt; for these forms have not been built up from fixed properties. "Properties" and "structures" are factors which empirical observation makes known to us to the extent that the same determinations and relationships return ever and again over long stretches of time. This kind of sameness of way and form is unknown to myth. For it, the world can assume a new face at any moment; for it is the emotion of the moment which determines this facial expression. In love and hate, in hope and fear, in joy and terror the features of reality are transformed. Any one of these emotions can give rise to a God-of-the-moment in a new mythical configuration.[4]

As philosophy and science oppose a genuine form of action to this mythical reaction, as they develop an independent mode of observation, or "theory," they see themselves forced to the very opposite extreme. They must endeavor to stop up the source from which myth forever takes its nourishment, by disputing every claim of the perception of expression. Science constructs a world in which expression-qualities—the "characteristics" of the trustworthy, or the fruitful, the friendly or the terrifying—are initially replaced with pure *sense qualities,* with colors, tones, and the like. And even these must be still further reduced. They are only "secondary" properties, based on primary properties, i.e., purely quantitative determinations. These primary properties constitute for cognition all that remains as objective reality. This is the conclusion drawn by physics. And, to the extent that philosophy holds to no other testimony than that of physics, it can go no further. Strict "physicalism" not only declares all proofs which have been advanced for the existence of "other selves" to be unattainable or invalid; it has even denied that it makes any sense to ask questions concerning a world other than that of the "it"—a world of the "you." Thus, not only the answer but

4. Cf. here my *Language and Myth,* trans. Susanne K. Langer (New York: Dover Publications, 1946).

even the question is mythical rather than philosophical and must hence be eradicated without compromise.[5]

If philosophy were nothing but the critique of knowledge, and if it were allowed to limit the concept of knowledge so as to encompass only "exact" science, then we could be satisfied with this conclusion. The language of physics would then be the only "inter-subjective language," and all that does not measure up to it falls out of our view of the world, as mere illusion. As Carnap puts it: "We demand of science that it not only have subjective meaning but be patent and valid for other minds. Science is the system of inter-subjectively valid statements. If our interpretation, that physicalistic language is the only inter-subjective language, is correct, it follows that physicalistic language is the language of science."[6] This language is not only inter-subjective it is also universal, i.e., each of its sentences is translatable; what is untranslatable comes to nothing whatever. If this position is assumed, then, for one thing, a language-*science* [itself] would exist only to the extent that "speech" manifests itself in phenomena of precise physical determinations, such as could be described by phonetics and the physiology of sound. That, on the contrary, language is "expression," that the "psychic" reveals itself in it, that, e.g., wishes, commands, and questions correspond to as many psychic states—all this would then be just as incapable of substantiation as the existence of "other selves."

The same would hold *a fortiori* for the science of art, the science of religion, and all the other "cultural sciences"—

5. Cf. Rudolf Carnap, *Scheinprobleme in der Philosophie: Das Fremdpsychologische und der Realismusstreit* (Berlin: Weltkreis Verlag, 1928).

6. Cf. Rudolf Carnap, "Physicalische Sprache als Universalsprache der Wissenschaft," *Erkenntnis,* II (1932), 441 ff.

insofar as they seek to be more than the representation of physical things and the play of change within these. The history of religion might perhaps concern itself then with the modes of behavior which we call rite and cult, prayer and sacrifice. It could define the manner and course of these actions with the utmost exactness, but it would have to withhold all judgment as to its "meaning": it would possess no criterion by which it could distinguish these "holy actions" from others falling into the realm of the "profane." The fact that this is a question concerning social rather than individual behavior does not help matters in the least, for knowledge of social action is bound by the same conditions. Such description could have only the validity of a purely behavioristic representation. It would show us what happens in certain human groups under fixed conditions. But if we do not wish to be the victims of a mere appearance, we must, in each judgment of these actions, carefully ask ourselves what it "means," i.e., what mental representation, thought, or feeling finds its echo in these phenomena.

But this negative conclusion at once implies a positive insight. It cannot be denied that "physicalism" has given rise to an important clarification of the problem, that it has *seen,* as such, one of the factors on which we were obliged to lay stress in distinguishing the humanities from the natural sciences. But instead of unraveling the Gordean knot it has cut it. The solution of the problem in its true universality can be attained only by a phenomenological analysis. Without reservation or epistemological dogma, we must seek to understand each sort of language in its uniqueness—the language of science, the language of art, of religion, etc. We must seek to determine what each contributes to the building up of a "common world." It is certain

that knowledge of physical things constitutes the foundation and substratum for every other construction of this
kind. There is no purely "ideal entity" that can dispense
with this support. The ideal exists only insofar as it presents
itself sensuously and materially in some manner and em-
bodies itself in this presentation. Religion, language, art—
these are never intelligible for us except in the monuments
which they themselves have produced. They are the tokens,
memorials, and reminders in which alone a religious, linguistic, or artistic meaning can be captured. This very embodiment constitutes the locus in which we come to know
the cultural object.

Like every other object, an object of culture has its place
in space and time. It has its here-and-now. It comes to be
and passes away. Insofar as we describe this here-and-now,
this coming-to-be and passing-away, we have no need to go
beyond the sphere of physical determinants. But, on the
other hand, in this description even the physical itself is
seen in a new *function*. It not only "is" and "becomes"; for
in this being and becoming something else "emerges."
What emerges is a "meaning," which is not absorbed by
what is merely physical, but is embodied upon and within
it; it is the factor common to all that content which we des-
ignate as "culture." To be sure, nothing prevents us from
ignoring this factor, making us blind to its "symbolic value"
through such a leaving-out and overlooking mode of abstraction. We can focus attention upon the composition of
the marble of Michelangelo's *David;* we can look upon
Raphael's *The School of Athens* as nothing but a canvas
covered with flecks of color of determinate quality and
spacial arrangement. At such a moment the work has become a thing among things and knowledge of it is subject
to the same conditions that hold for any other space-time

existent [*Dasein*]. But the moment we become absorbed in the *presentation* and abandon ourselves to it, the difference has emerged once again.

But always we discern in a work of art two fundamental factors, which constitute the whole of the work only by means of their union and interpenetration. The colors in Raphael's painting have a "presentation-function" only insofar as they suggest an object. Here we do not lose ourselves in sheer observation of the colors; we do not see them *as* colors; instead, it is through these colors that we see what is objective—a definite scene, a conversation between two philosophers. But even what is objective in this sense is not the unique, the true subject matter of the painting. The painting is not merely the presentation of an historical scene, a conversation between Plato and Aristotle. For in reality it is not Plato and Aristotle who speak to us here but Raphael himself. These three dimensions— the physical thereness [*Dasein*], the object-presentation, and the evidence of a unique personality—are determining and indispensable in anything that is a genuine "work" ["*Werk*"] and not merely a "result" ["*Wirkung*"] and of all that in this sense belongs not only to "nature" but also to "culture." The exclusion of one of these three dimensions, confinement within a single plane of observation, always yields only a surface image of culture, revealing none of its genuine depth.

Strict positivism is given to denying this depth because it is afraid of losing itself in its obscurity. And it must be admitted that, when one compares expression-perception with thing-perception, an extraordinary difficulty and inconceivability appears to be inherent to expression-perception. But this inconceivability does not exist for the naive world view. Without reserve it entrusts itself to the study of expression and feels completely at home with it. No theoretical argument can shake it in its conviction.

But all this changes as soon as reflection begins to concern itself with the problem. All logical "proofs" for the existence of other selves which have been pursued in the history of philosophy have failed and all psychological explanations that have been given are uncertain and questionable. It is not hard to see through the defect of these proofs and explanations.[7] Skepticism is always able to find the weak point against which to launch its attacks. In the second edition of the *Critique of Pure Reason* Kant added a special refutation of "psychological idealism." By means of this refutation he was determined, as he said, to remove from "philosophy and common human reason the scandal" of being forced to accept the existence of external things merely on faith.[8] This scandal becomes all the more violent when we turn from the question of external things to that of other subjects. Indeed, metaphysical dogmatists—themselves opposed to it, but unable to explain it—have become convinced that at this point the skeptical arguments are decisive; they have regarded this doubt as irrefutable, though obviously untenable. Schopenhauer says that theoretical egoism which holds all appearances external to oneself to be mere phantoms can be refuted by countless arguments.

But anyone convinced of this in all seriousness is to be found only in an insane asylum: in which case, what is needed is not so much a proof as a cure. Here, to be sure, solipsism may be viewed as a small frontier fortress, which may prove increasingly invincible, but whose garrison is absolutely unable to get out, and which we may pass and

7. Cf. *Philosophy of Symbolic Forms*, III, 80 ff.
8. Immanuel Kant, *Critique of Pure Reason*, trans. N. K. Smith (London: The Macmillan Co., 1950), pp. 34–36.

turn our backs on without danger.[9] But philosophy is surely in an unsatisfactory state of affairs, if it must appeal here to "healthy minds" in order to criticize and keep under control what is otherwise one of its supreme tasks.

It is clear that the process of substantiation cannot go on into infinity, that at last we must strike on something that is not deductively demonstrable but which can only be pointed out. This holds as well for knowledge of one's own ego as of knowledge of the external world. Even the *cogito ergo sum* is, as Descartes emphasized again and again, no formal argument but a purely intuitive cognition. In the area of the really basic problems we cannot leave sole authority to reflection. Here we must fall back on sources of knowledge of a different and more original kind. What must be demanded is that the phenomena give rise to no internal contradictions, once we have moved them into the clear light of reflection, that they harmonize with each other. But this requirement is certainly not fulfilled if the "natural" view of the world irresistibly forces us to the argument that theory itself must be defined as senseless or as absolutely incapable of being grounded.

It is often held, as an all but self-evident assumption, in need of no further proof, that all entities immediately accessible to knowledge are determinate physical data. In which case, the sensuously given—color, sound, feelings of touch and temperature, smell, and taste—are the only things capable of immediate experience. All else, especially spiritual existence, may indeed be implied by this primary data, but for this very reason it remains uncertain. Yet phenomenological analysis is far from substantiating this

9. Arthur Schopenhauer, *The World as Will and Representation,* trans. E.F.J. Payne (Indian Hills: Falcon's Wing Press, 1958), Bk. II, par. 19.

assumption. Neither functional nor genetic observation justifies us in giving sense perception primacy over expression-perception. With regard to the purely genetic account, ontogeny as well as phylogeny—the development of consciousness in the individual as well as in the species—shows us that the very data which, above all, were thought to be the starting points of all knowledge of reality, are relatively late products and that a grueling and lengthy process of abstraction is necessary in order to draw them out from the whole of human experience. All unbiased psychological observation testifies to the fact that the first experiences of the child are experiences of expression.[10] The perception of "things" and "thing qualities" comes into its own only much later. It is *language,* above all, that first turns the tide. For the capacity for objective representation grows in direct ratio as we [begin to] give linguistic expression to our experience of the world, instead of only experiencing it through passive impressions.[11] Still, the fact that all linguistic expression is and remains "metaphorical" expression is proof that the capacity for objective representation can never become completely dominant in the domain of language. Metaphor constitutes an indispensable factor in language in its organic wholeness. Without metaphor language would lose its lifeblood and stiffen into a conventional system of signs.

But even the genuinely *theoretical* view of the world, the world view of philosophy and science, by no means begins by regarding the world as a sum total of merely "physical" things. The interpretation of the cosmos as a system

10. Cf. *Philosophy of Symbolic Forms,* III, 64 ff.

11. For more detailed treatment see my article, "Le language et la construction du monde des objets," *Journal de Psychologie Normale et Pathologique,* XXX (1933), 18–44. Trans. by P. Guillaume.

of bodies and the interpretation of events as a result of purely physical forces did not emerge until late; it can hardly be traced further back than the seventeenth century. Plato begins one of his proofs for the immortality of the soul with the view that the soul is the "beginning of all motion," arguing that without the soul the world would come to a standstill. With Aristotle this thought becomes the starting point of cosmology. If the heavenly bodies sustain a perpetual motion, this fact can only have its ground in a soul, as the principle from which this motion takes its rise. Even Giordano Bruno, herald and prophet of the new Copernican conception of the universe, declares that the doctrine that the heavens are animate is a conviction on which all philosophers agree.

With Descartes we encounter for the first time the notion of a strictly mathematical and mechanical universe. And from this point onward its expanding grasp is irresistible. But it is clear that this view of things is terminal, not initial. It is a product of abstraction, which science sees itself forced to resort to in its efforts to account for and gain mastery of the phenomena of nature. Through it, as Descartes himself has stated, man seeks to make himself "master and possessor of nature" *(maître et possesseur de la nature).* Thus the physical "nature" of things is that aspect of appearances which always recurs in the same manner and which, as such, admits of being reduced to strict unbroken laws. It is what we are able to extract as constant and abiding from the sum total of phenomena known to us. But what is thus loosened and extracted can only be the product of theoretical reflection. It is a *terminus ad quem,* not a *terminus a quo*—an end, not a beginning. Natural science, as such, should and must be free to determine its way to the attainment of this goal. Not only does it seek increasingly to suppress all that is "personal" it strives toward a conception of the world from which the "personal" has been eliminated.[12] It achieves its true aim only by disregarding the world of self and other.

The astronomical world appears to have been the first to achieve its supreme triumph and ultimate success through this mode of observation. With Kepler the conception of "animate planets" (even though initially it dominated his work) begins to be pushed ever further into the background the more he advances toward a truly mathematical theory of planetary motion. And with Galileo the theory of planetary animation is declared to be a pure fiction. Recent philosophy has pushed still further in this direction. It demands the elimination of "occult" psychic qualities, not only from astronomy and physics, but from all natural events. Even biology must not hold back; even for it, the dominance of "vitalism" appears to have come to an end. Thus life is not only expelled from the inorganic, it is also banished from organic nature. Even the organism is subject to the laws of mechanics, the laws of pressure and impact, and without qualification.

All attempts to oppose this radical "devitalization" of nature with metaphysical arguments have not only miscarried but have compromised the very cause they have sought to serve. Gustav Theodor Fechner made such an attempt in the nineteenth century. He was himself a physicist and was determined to open the way to a psycho-

12. In an interesting article Schroedinger has set forth the argument that this elimination of the "personal" can never be *absolutely* successful, that it is to be viewed as only a limiting concept of scientific method. Cf. Schroedinger, "Quelques remarques au sujet des basis de la connaissance scientific," *Scientia,* LVII (March 1935), 181–91.

physics within the field of psychology. But in the main his philosophical attempts to attack the mechanical conception of the universe at its roots came to nothing. To the "night-time view" of natural science he was determined to oppose the "daylight view." It is highly instructive for our purpose that we pursue the method which Fechner made use of here. It consists in nothing other than the fact that he starts with perception of expression and seeks to restore it to its full claims. According to Fechner this way of perceiving not only does not deceive, it is at bottom the only means by which we can free ourselves from the vicious circle of abstract thought and make contact with reality. Fechner undertook his boldest and most noteworthy venture in this direction in his *Nanna oder über das Seelenleben der Pflanzen* [Nanna: Or on the Psychic Life of Plants]. Here all phenomena whatsoever of the plant world are thought of as expression-phenomena and explained as such. For Fechner plants are "souls"—"souls which, quietly blooming and exhaling fragrance, fulfill a still higher yearning in the drawing of dew in their thirst, in the thrust of their budding drive, and in turning toward the light."[13] But the mechanical theory has never tired of reducing to "tropisms" all the phenomena in which Fechner sought to find proof of psychic life in plants; these can themselves be explained by means of known physical and chemical forces. According to the mechanical theory, heliotropism, geotropism, and phototropism are sufficient to account for the processes of plant life. The modern founders of the tropism theory have not hesitated to extend the theory to animal life. In doing so they have regarded themselves as having

13. G. T. Fechner, *Nanna*, 4th ed. (Hamburg und Leipzig: L. Voss, 1908), p. 10.

established strict empirical proof for Descartes' theory that animals are automatons.[14]

Finally it appears that *psychology* itself cannot provide the stopping point to this continual objectification and mechanization. Even Descartes' *cogito* no longer constitutes a fixed and unscalable wall. For Descartes himself it signified a sharp dividing line between "nature" and "mind" for it was the expression of "pure thought." But is there such pure thought? Or is what we have taken to be "pure thought," perhaps a mere construction, a rationalization? The attempt to carry through the thesis of radical empiricism with full precision must necessarily lead to this question.

One of the keenest modern analysts of psychology has addressed himself to this very problem. In his *Essays in Radical Empiricism* William James has raised the question as to whether there is any experiential evidence for what we commonly refer to as "consciousness." And he arrives at a negative conclusion: psychology must learn to give up the concept of consciousness, just as it learned to get along without the concept of a soul substance. But, in fact the two are but two characterizations of one and the same problem. According to James, the statement that there is a "pure thought," a "pure self-consciousness," a "transcendental unity of apperception," is simply vacuous. It refers to no demonstrable psychological fact. It is a mere echo, a reverberation which the metaphysical soul substance in its disappearance has left behind. For there is no self-consciousness and no feeling of self without determinate body feeling. "I am as confident," writes James, "as I am of anything that, in myself, the stream of thinking (which I recognize

14. Cf. Jacques Loeb, *The Dynamics of Living Matter* (New York: Columbia University Press, 1906).

emphatically as a phenomenon) is only a careless name for what, when scrutinized, reveals itself to consist chiefly of the stream of my breathing. The 'I think' which Kant said must be able to accompany all my objects is the 'I breathe' which actually does accompany them."[15]

From the standpoint of a strict empiricism, concerned solely with establishing the facts of consciousness, the *concept* of self-consciousness of the classical idealist tradition appears to be questionable. James is quick to add that this dubiousness does not attach to the phenomenon as such but only to a fixed notion regarding it. If he disputes the fact of a "pure self-consciousness," it is only insofar as this term is thought to refer to an enduring thing in itself. What he denies is only the substantial nature of the self, not its *functional* meaningfulness. As he says explicitly, "Let me immediately explain that I mean only to deny that the word stands for an entity, but to insist most emphatically that it stands for a function."

If we hold firmly to this statement of the problem, the question as to relation of the "I" and the "you" at once appears in a new light. For now they can no longer be described as independent things or essences, as things in themselves, separated, so to speak, by a spacial gulf across which nevertheless there occurs some kind of effect at a distance, an *actio in distans*. Instead, the "I" and the "you" exist only insofar as they exist "for each other," only insofar as they stand in the functional relation of being reciprocally conditioned.

The fact of civilization is itself the most striking expres-

15. William James, "Does Consciousness Exist?", *Essays in Radical Empiricism* (New York: Longmans, Green and Co., 1912), pp. 36 f. Cf. also Bertrand Russell, *The Analysis of Mind* (New York: The Macmillan Co., 1921).

sion and incontrovertible proof of this reciprocal conditioning. As a matter of principle, civilization by no means
falls outside the province of scientific modes of observation
which treat of things and the relations of things. Civilization and its study do not constitute a "state within a state."
For its artifacts are physical and material. The individuals
who create these works have their own psychic existence
and life peculiarities. These all can and must be studied
under physical, psychological, and sociological categories.

But the moment we turn from particular works and individuals to the *forms* of culture and abandon ourselves to
contemplation of them, we stand on the crest of a new
problem. Strict naturalism does not deny the existence of
this problem. But it believes itself able to master this "state
within a state" by attempting to explain these forms—the
forms of language, art, and religion—as simple *sum totals*
of individual effects. Language is said to be a convention,
"something agreed upon," which the individuals simply
encounter; political and social life is traced back to a "social
contract." The circular nature of such arguments is obvious.
For agreement is possible only in the medium of speech
and, similarly, a contract has meaning and force only
within a state and a medium of laws. The first question to
be resolved here is that of determining the locus of this
medium and its conditions. Metaphysical theories about
the origin of language, religion, and society answer this
question by tracing the origin of language and society to
supra-personal powers, to the workings of the *"Volksgeist"*
or the *"Kulturseele."* But this means forsaking scientific
explanation and a fall back into myth. Here the world of
culture is explained as a kind of over-world, which works
itself out in the physical world and in the lives of human
beings.

A critical philosophy of culture cannot surrender to either type of explanation. It must avoid both the Scylla of naturalism and the Charybdis of metaphysics. The course becomes plain as soon as it is understood that the "I" and the "you" are not finished *data* which create these forms of culture through the influence they exercise on each other. Instead, it is only within and by virtue of these forms that the two spheres, the world of the "I" and that of the "you" *come into being.* There is no fixed, self-enclosed "I," which in association with a similar "you" seeks to penetrate into its sphere as if from outside. Again and again, thorough analysis has shown that, starting with this assumption, the goal is unattainable. On such an assumption, it is the same in the spiritual realm as in the world of matter: each entity is restricted to its particular locus and, as such, is impenetrable to any other entity. However, if we no longer begin with the "I" and the "you" as two substantially separate entities, but locate them in the meeting point of that reciprocal *transaction,* which consummates itself in speech or any other culture-form, our perplexities dissipate. In the beginning is the act: always, in the function of speech, in artistic creation, in the process of thought and inquiry there is expressed a specific *activity.* And only in this activity do the "I" and the "you" exist with the possibility of simultaneously distinguishing themselves from each other. They exist both within and next to each other as they preserve their unity within speech, thought, and all manner of artistic expression.

From this it is understandable—indeed, it seems little short of necessary—that the psychology of strict "behaviorism" must eventually turn the doubt which it has raised against the reality of the "you"—against the existence of "other selves"—against the reality of the "I" also, against

the *cogito* in the proper sense. For when the one factor falls
the other falls. Paradoxical as James' question, "Does Consciousness Exist?" may sound, it is at bottom only a logical
consequence [of his psychological assumptions]. But this
very consequence can show us the way out of the dilemma
by making clear to us the blind alley into which it has
strayed. Simply invoking the compelling force of expression-perception is not in itself sufficient to remove us from
this impasse. We must have recourse to still another argument; within what we term expression we must distinguish
two diverse factors. There is "expression of emotion" even
in the animal world. Charles Darwin has studied and described it minutely in one of his works. Still, all that we
are able to establish with respect to it is and remains *passive*
expression. But in the province of human existence and
human culture we immediately encounter something new.
For, diverse as they are from one another, all culture-forms
are *active expression-forms*. They are not mere reactions—
like blushing, frowning, or doubling of the fist—but genuine actions. They are not simply events which play themselves out within and upon our bodies, but are, as it were,
specific *energies*. It is through the exercise of these energies
that the world of culture takes form—the world of language, art, and religion.

To be sure, behaviorism believes itself prepared against
this objection. It stands firmly upon the ground of the
given. And it insists that the given is never for us anything
but a determinate association of sense qualities, a manifold
of colors, a succession of sounds. But if we maintain that
all these contents not only "exist" but that something else
"appears" in them, that in addition to their sheer physical
thereness a "symbolic value" is transmitted by them, we
go beyond what sense experience alone can tell us. Accord-

ing to Russell, "behaviorists say that the talk they have to listen to can be explained without supposing that people think. Where you might expect a chapter on 'thought processes' you come instead upon a chapter on 'The Language Habit.' It is humiliating to find how terribly adequate this hypothesis turns out to be."[16]

That a large part of daily speech justly deserves this scathing criticism can scarcely be disputed. But are we justified in extending this evaluation to all human speech? Does all of it merely follow the law of imitation and is it nothing but empty "parroting"? Is there no difference between the talking of the parrot and human speech? Russell himself advances a telling example in support of the behaviorist thesis. We are to suppose that a teacher in examining his students sets down a certain problem in arithmetic, for example, a problem in multiplication. From one student he gets a "correct" answer and from the other a "false" answer. But does this "correct" answer prove anything more than that a mere word-formula has stamped itself upon the memory of the student and that he is able to repeat it?

Now this is doubtless true; but no real teacher will proceed on the basis of an examination that merely asks for answers. He will find a way to bring the independence of his student into play. He will devise a problem which in all probability the student has never seen before. In this way he will come to know not only the measure of acquired knowledge the student possesses but also the degree to which he understands how to use it. With this, all reason for uncertainty is removed—uncertainty which, in principle, even the most elaborate but purely passive behavior

16. Bertrand Russell, *The Analysis of Mind* (London: George Allen & Unwin Ltd., 1921), pp. 26 f.

could not dispel. Surely there is passive speech, just as there
is passive expression. It does not go beyond mere "language
habit." But true speech, meaningful *"logos,"* is something
different in kind. It is never purely imitative, it is productive. And only in this productive function, only within this
latent energy does it give evidence for and display that
other energy which we call "thinking."

The true relationship between "I" and "you" has its
being in the act of sharing a common universe of discourse.
It is continual daily engagement in this common language-
world that gives rise to the "I-you" relationship. To be sure,
this circumstance has a negative as well as a positive import
and evaluation. It is an age-old complaint that speech not
only brings us together but also divides us. Philosophy,
mysticism, and poetry have reiterated this complaint again
and again.

> Warum kann der lebendige Geist dem Geist
> nicht erscheinen?
> Spricht die Seele, so spricht, ach,
> schon die Seele nicht mehr![17]

Still, this yearning for a direct contemplation in thought
and feeling, which could dispense with all symbolism and
mediation, rests on a self-deception. It would only be justified if the world of the "I" were a given, finished, and
enduring entity, if words and images had no other task than
to *transport* this givenness from one subject to another.
But this interpretation does not do justice to the true
import and depth of the processes of speech and artistic
creation. If the function of language and art were only

17. [Why is one living mind never directly present to another?
When the soul speaks, alas, it is no longer the soul that speaks!]

that of building bridges between the inner worlds of different subjects, the objection that this task is utopian would be justified. Such an abyss cannot be filled; in the end such a world belongs only to itself and knows only itself.

But the true relation is quite otherwise. In speech and art the individuals not only share what they already possess; it is only by virtue of this sharing process in speech and art that individuals have attained what they possess. This can be observed in any living and meaningful conversation. It is never simply a question of imparting information, but of statement and response. It is only in this twofold process that true thought emerges. Plato has said that "questioning and answering each other in discourse" is our only access to the world of the "idea." In question and answer "I" and "you" must be distinguished, not only that they may understand each other, but even if each is ever to know himself. Here both factors are in continual interplay. The thought of one partner is kindled by that of another. And by virtue of this interaction each constructs for himself a "shared world" of meaning *within the medium of language*. Wherever this medium fails us our own grasp becomes unsure and dubious. All thought must prove itself in language. Even the force and depth of feeling first shows and proves itself *in* the expression of feeling. We have all had the experience, characteristic of the "unformulated" thought of dreams, of being capable of some extraordinary feat. Effortlessly, we may have come upon the solution to some difficult problem. But the moment we awake the solution dissolves. The necessity of putting the achievement into words shows us its shadowy vacuousness. Thus, language is *not merely* an *externalization* of ourselves; like art and each of the other "symbolic forms," it is a *pathway to* [the realization of] ourselves. It is productive in the sense that consciousness and knowledge of ourselves is first achieved by means of it.

What is constantly required here is the twofold method of synthesis and analysis, separation and reintegration. This "dialectic" is apparent not only in true dialogue but even in a monologue. For even thinking to oneself is, as Plato has remarked, a "conversation of the soul with itself." Paradoxical as it may sound, there is good reason for saying that in the monologue the function which predominates is *division* of self, whereas in the dialogue it is *reintegration* that is central. For the "conversation of the soul with itself" is only possible by virtue of the fact that in the process the soul in a sense undergoes a division within itself. It must undertake both the function of speaking and that of hearing, of questioning and answering. To this extent the soul ceases to be purely singular, purely an "individual." It becomes a "person" in the basic etymological meaning of the word, which goes back to the mask and the role of the player on the stage. Thus, according to Vossler,

> The concept of the individual does not take account of this possibility; for, as such, it remains indivisible. If human beings were nothing but individuals and not persons also, conversation would be unintelligible, for it consists in splitting and reunifying the soul. . . . In the final analysis, i.e., when considered philosophically, the real vehicle and creator of conversation is always a single person, who can divide into at least two and finally into any number of characters or sub-persons.[18]

18. Karl Vossler, *The Spirit of Language in Civilization,* trans. Oscar Oeser (London: Kegan Paul, Trench, Trubner & Co., Ltd., 1932), p. 12.

This double function of all symbolism, the function of division and reintegration, emerges still more clearly and convincingly in art. "There is no surer way to escape the world than through art, and there is no surer way to tie oneself to it than through art." These words of Goethe give expression to a basal feeling at work in every great artist. The artist possesses the strongest will and the strongest capacity for communication. He cannot gain rest or peace till he has discovered how to bring to life in others all that lives in himself. And yet it is just in this continual self-renewing flow of communication that the artist feels himself isolated and thrown back within the limits of his own ego. For no single work that he creates can capture the fullness of this vision. Always there remains an evident and distressing opposition: "outer" and "inner" never completely correspond. But these restrictions, which the artist must acknowledge, do not stop his efforts. He continues to create for he knows that it is only by doing so that he can discover and gain possession of his own self. His world and his true self can be had only in the shape which he gives to them.

In religious feeling, too, we find the same duplexity. The deeper and more inward the feeling the more it *appears* to spurn the world and break all ties, all social realities binding man to man. Here the believer knows only himself and God and does not want to know anything else. *"Deum animamque scire cupio,"* says Augustine, *"nihilne plus? Nihil omnino."* And yet, with Augustine, as with every other religious genius, the power of his belief first proves itself in being made public. He must communicate his belief to others, he must fill them with his own religious passion and fervor, in order to be certain of his belief. This is possible only by means of religious constructs—constructs which begin as symbols and end as dogmas. Thus, even here, every initial expression of feeling is already the beginning of an alienation. It is the destiny and, in a sense, the immanent tragedy of every spiritual form that it can never overcome this inner tension; to extinguish it is to extinguish the life of the spirit. For the life of spirit consists in this very act of severing what is whole in order that what has been severed may be even more securely united.

CHAPTER 3

Nature-Concepts
and Culture-Concepts

WE BEGAN WITH the premise that all attempts to fix the limits between "natural science" and "the humanities" will remain unsatisfactory and inadequate until we resolve to carry the discussion beyond the domain of pure logic and the theoretical sciences. To determine this distinction with precision, it is necessary to go beyond the structure of concepts to the structure of perception. As we sought to show, perception already contains in germinal form that opposition which emerges in explicit form in the opposed methods of natural science and the humanities. Today it is generally agreed that, regardless of one's epistemological persuasion, one cannot take issue with the premise that any concept which claims to give us knowledge of reality must, in the final analysis, find its validation in perception. This statement holds not only for concepts of particulars; it holds also for the various *concepts of classes* which we encounter in the development of science. If these classes are not mere fictions, if they are taken to signify something more than arbitrary names which we have created only in the interest of classification, then they must possess a *fundamentum in re*. It must be possible to trace them back to their ultimate epistemological origins.

Here, too, it must be possible to show that the distinction at issue is based on an ultimate twofold tendency within intuition and perception. Having won a firm foothold in this sphere, we must take up our initial question once again. We must return to logic and investigate the *logical character* of *culture-concepts*. Even the most fleeting observation shows us that they possess such a character, that even manifold as they are and divergent as are the objects to which they refer, they are all united by a single "spiritual bond." But what sort of bond is this? To what family do these concepts belong? And what is the relation between them and other classes of concepts?

Until now three fundamentally different answers have been given to this question. The contest and clash of diverse tendencies, which even yet are struggling for dominance of the modern theory of science, are mirrored in these answers. Here it is natural science, history, and psychology that are in competition. Each comes forward with a thoroughly grounded claim, which demands a continual hearing. Even from this it is evident that the problem cannot be solved simply by dogmatic decree. Each one of the three tendencies can withdraw to a position upon which it can base itself with certainty and from which it cannot be dislodged by any arguments from its opponents. For the physical, the psychic, and the historical do in fact belong of necessity to concepts of cultural objects. They are the three factors from which it is constructed. A cultural object continually demands a physical-material substratum. The painting is captured in the canvas, the statue in the marble, the historical document in inscriptions which we find written on parchment or paper. A bygone civilization presents itself to us only in such documents and monuments. But if all these *physical* artifacts are to be correctly read and understood, they require at one and the same time a double interpretation. Each must be placed historically; it must be studied with respect to period and origin—but it must also be understood as the expression of definite spiritual attitudes, which in some manner are capable of being re-experienced by us. Thus physical, historical, and psychological concepts are continually entering into the description of a cultural object. But our problem does not concern the content of these concepts themselves; it concerns the *synthesis* by virtue of which we order them into a new whole —a whole which exists *sui generis*. Every mode of inquiry which fails to do justice to this synthesis is inadequate. For, in advancing to a determinate level of conceptualization, everything depends on the particular manner in which these ideas are unified and tied together. Although the argument that every cultural object manifests a physical, a psychological, and an historical aspect is incontrovertible, its specific meaning as cultural object still remains concealed from us so long as we treat these factors in isolation, instead of grasping them in their reciprocal interrelation, their mutual "penetration." Each of these aspects—physical, psychological, and historical—is necessary; but no one of them can yield the total image which is our concern in the humanities.

Here, to be sure, we encounter a difficulty which is bound up with the present state of logic and with its historical development. We have possessed a logic of mathematics since Plato and a logic of biology since Aristotle. With them the mathematical concepts of relation and the biological concepts of genus and species were given their secure places. The logic of the mathematical science of nature was developed by Descartes, Leibniz, and Kant. Finally, in the nineteenth century we see the emergence of the first attempts at a "logic of history." If, on the other hand, we look for the fundamental concepts of the sciences of language, art, and religion, we are struck by the fact that, to a certain degree, they are still wrapped in mystery: they have not found their "natural place" within the system of logic.

I prefer to set forth the actual state of affairs by means of concrete examples drawn directly from work within the humanities, rather than to establish it through abstract arguments. Actual research in this area has continually gone its own way; it has not subjected itself to that Procrustean bed of precise conceptual distinctions into which people have so often sought to force it for the sake of logic or epistemology. Here, better than anywhere else, we are able to read off the true nature of the problem. Each of the humanistic disciplines develops determinate concepts of form and style and uses them in arriving at a systematic survey, a classification and differentiation of the phenomena with which it concerns itself. These concepts of form are neither "nomothetic" nor "idiographic." They are not nomothetic for their function is not to establish general laws from which the individual phenomena can be deductively inferred. But neither do they admit of being reduced to historical inquiry. This is particularly clear in linguistics. It is indeed a well established fact that, wherever possible, language must be studied in its development and that this procedure yields the most fruitful and the richest of information. Nevertheless, in order to survey thoroughly the value of such inquiry and explanation, in order to take in the totality of the linguistic phenomena, it is necessary to proceed in a different way.

We must begin with what Wilhelm von Humboldt called the "inner form of language" and attempt to gain an insight into the articulation of this inner form of language. Our concern here is with the purely *structural problems* of language, which are obviously distinct from historical problems and which can and must be treated separately. The structure of a language can be determined even when we know little or nothing of its historical development. Thus Humboldt was the first to establish the concept of "poly-synthetic languages" and, in its description, he gave a striking example of the analysis of language-structure. Here there were no available dates of origin and development. A similar circumstance always prevails where we are dealing with languages of pre-literate peoples. In his *Comparative Grammar of the Bantu Languages* Carl Meinhof has investigated the peculiarities of these languages, which, instead of handling the declension of nouns according to so-called "natural genders"—masculine, feminine, and neuter—employ wholly different principles of classification.[1] Again in this analysis, historical factors have not come into play; nor does their absence jeopardize the certainty of our understanding of the structure of language.

Let us shift our attention from linguistics to another major field of the humanities—to the study of art [*Kunst-wissenschaft*]. To attempt to bridge the two fields may appear at first sight to be an extremely rash undertaking, for in terms of the objects with which they concern themselves and in their respective methods they appear to be far apart. Nevertheless, they employ concepts which are related in their general form and which belong, at it were, to the same logical "family." Art history, too, is unable to develop when it seeks to limit itself exclusively to historical observations and the retelling of what has been and what has

1. For more details see my *Philosophy of Symbolic Forms.*

come to be. Here, too, the Platonic thesis holds good: that there can be no knowledge of becoming as *mere* becoming. If these sciences are to gain a foothold in becoming, if they are to be able to survey and control it, it is necessary first that they secure themselves upon fixed points of support within "being." All historical knowledge implies determinate knowledge of a "form" and "essence" as its frame of reference.

This correlation and interpenetration of the two factors [being and becoming] emerges with ever increasing clarity as scientific research finds itself forced to reflect upon its own methods. It emerges with particular clarity in a work like Heinrich Wölfflin's *Fundamental Concepts of Art History*. Wölfflin is determined to carefully avoid all speculation; he thinks and speaks as a pure empiricist. Nevertheless, he insists emphatically that the facts themselves must remain mute unless we have previously established determinate conceptual frames of reference with respect to which they are to be ordered and interpreted. It is just this which he sees as the need which his book will fulfill. "Conceptual research," he explains in the foreword, "has not kept pace with factual research." Wölfflin's work is not meant strictly as art history. It is presented as the "prolegomena to any future art history" capable of developing as a science. At one point he insists, "We are not giving the history of the painterly style; we are seeking the general concept."[2] This becomes known and established by means of the fact that *painterly* style is clearly and definitely set apart from *linear* style and opposed to it in all the forms in which it manifests itself. For Wölfflin the "linear" and the "painterly" oppose each other as two modes of vision. They

2. Heinrich Wölfflin, *Principles of Art History*, trans. M. D. Hotlinger (New York: Dover Publications Inc., 1950), p. 31.

are two ways of comprehending spacial relations; they are intent upon two completely diverse goals and each, consequently, always selects a particular aspect of things in space. The "linear" distills itself into the firm plastic forms of things; the painterly is exhausted in its appearance. "The one is a fixed shape, the other is a changing appearance; the one is enduring form, measurable and limited, whereas the other exists as motion or functional form; in the one we have things in themselves, in the other things in interaction."[3]

It is self-evident that Wölfflin would not have been able to formulate this contrast between "linear" and "painterly" and bring it to intuitive clarity if he had not supported himself step by step upon an enormous amount of historical visual data. On the other hand, he insists emphatically that what his analysis seeks to achieve constitutes no single historical event conditioned by and limited to a definite point in time. Wölfflin's basic concepts are no more "idiographic" than were those of Humboldt. They are based upon completely general circumstances. But, in contrast to the general concepts of class and law in natural science, they present universals of another kind and level.

By means of definite historical phenomena—in the contrast between the form-language of the Classic period and that of the Baroque, the contrast between the sixteenth and the seventeenth centuries, between Dürer and Rembrandt —a fundamental difference of form is thought to have been brought to consciousness. The individual manifestations are not meant to be taken as paradigmatic illustrations of this distinction; and in no sense are they taken as the ground for this distinction. For Wölfflin there is a "classic"

3. *Ibid.*

and a "baroque" not only in the history of modern times
but also in the architecture of antiquity and in even so
heterogeneous a style as Gothic.[4] Nor does the distinction
admit of being understood by being traced back to national
or individual differences. Such differences do play a role
in the development of linear and painterly styles. But the
mode of existence characteristic of these styles cannot be
deduced from such factors. On the contrary, it is something
which can be clearly and intuitively realized in the most
divergent of epochs and national cultures. Even the question as to the *development* of one style from another can
be raised and answered independently of these premises,
according to Wölfflin. The history of style cannot proceed
beyond a determinate and fundamental layer of concepts
which refer to the "presentation as such": "a history of the
development of seeing in the West could be written for
which variations of individual and national character
would cease to be of any importance."[5] There is a style
which, essentially objective in outlook, seeks to catch and
highlight things in their solid, tangible relations, and, on
the contrary, there is a style which, more subjective in at-
titude, bases its presentation on the appearance, in which
what is visible appears real to the eye. . . ."[6] The more ver-
satile artists are able to work in both styles. At one point
in his work Wölfflin says, "Naturally, for purposes of illus-
tration, we could only proceed by referring to the individual work of art, but everything that was said of Raphael
and Titian, of Rembrandt and Velazquez, was only intended to elucidate the general continuity, but not to set

4. Wölfflin, p. 221.
5. Wölfflin, p. 12.
6. Wölfflin, p. 20.

forth the special value of the selected works."[7] In this Wölfflin also sets forth the ideal of a history of art which would be a "history of art without names."[8] It requires no names because it is concerned not with particulars but with principles and to this extent with something "anonymous" —with the changes in spacial *vision* and with the consequent modifications in the eye's feel for space and form.

Thus it is extremely interesting and important for the logician to note how Wölfflin, by enunciating pure *concepts of structure* in the science of art, has been led involuntarily to completely universal problems of the "science of form." It is no accident that he has resorted to expressions which reach beyond the sphere of art and have relevance for linguistics. Again and again Humboldt emphasized that the difference between particular languages is no mere difference in "sounds and markings." Instead, for him, a unique "world view," a definite and fundamental direction of thought and representation, is expressed in each language-type. A thoroughly analogous thought is basic for Wölfflin, though, with him, to be sure, there is no immediate dependence or link to Humboldt's world of thought. He transports the same principle from the world of thought and representation to the world of intuition and vision. As he states emphatically, each artistic style characterizes itself, not only according to certain formal factors—the manner of sketching, the contours, etc.—but in each of these factors there is expressed a definite total orientation, a mental predisposition of the eyes, so to speak. Such differences are not mere matters of taste: "conditioned and conditioning, they contain the foundation of the total

7. Wölfflin, p. 226.
8. Wölfflin, p. 12.

world view of a people."[9] Just as different languages deviate from one another in their grammars and syntax, so, the language of art changes in grammar and syntax with the transition from linear to painterly. It is not into one unchanging form that the content of the world crystalizes for intuition.[10] To trace this change in the form of intuition and to make its inner logic intelligible is one of the major tasks of the science of art.

But here we meet another problem. We have said that the concepts of form and style in the humanities, as well as the concepts in the natural sciences, are clearly distinct from historical concepts, that they present a class of concepts which are *sui generis*. But do they, perhaps, admit of being reduced to concepts of still another type—to concepts of value? The role which concepts of value play in Rickert's logic of history is well known. Rickert has emphatically insisted that the science of history is not concerned solely with establishing individual facts, but that it must set forth a connection between them, and that this historical synthesis is neither feasible nor possible without reference to a "universal." But in place of the concepts of being in the natural sciences he introduces a system of value concepts for history and the humanities. Accordingly, the mass of historical materials cannot be systematized nor can historical knowledge be made accessible except by relating particulars to universal (trans-historical) values. But even *this* thesis does not hold up under the more exacting examination of the concrete state of affairs in the humanities. For there is a radical difference between style-concepts and value-concepts. What style-concepts present is not an ought but simply an "is"—even though this "is" is not concerned with

9. Wölfflin, p. 237.
10. Wölfflin, p. 226.

physical things but with the persistence of "forms." When I speak of the "form" of a language, or of a definite art "form," this, *in itself*, has nothing to do with value reference.

It is possible for the establishment of such forms to be *linked* to judgments of value, but they are not constitutive of the understanding of the form as such, of its intention and meaning. Thus, for example, Humboldt, in his studies into the development of human speech, thought he could establish a certain intellectual "hierarchy" among linguistic forms. He sees the culmination of this hierarchy in inflected languages. He attempts to prove that the method of inflection is ultimately the "only lawful form," that it is not completely achieved by the isolating, agglutinative, or polysynthetic languages. He distinguishes between languages having this "lawful form" and those which deviate from it in one way or another.[11] But clearly he was only able to undertake this ranking of languages after first establishing their structural differences in accordance with definite principles, and this must take place in complete independence of any kind of value assumptions.

The same holds for the style-concepts of the science of art. Here, too, we can rank one style above another on the basis of aesthetic norms which we believe to be certain. But we do not grasp the "what" of the particular style—its particularity and its character—on the basis of such normative concepts. Instead, we rely on other criteria for its definition. When Wölfflin speaks of "classic" and "baroque," these two concepts have for him merely a descriptive, not an aesthetically qualitative, or normative, significance. Connotations of the excellent or paradigmatic are by no means attributed

11. Wilhelm von Humboldt, "Einleitung zum Kawi-Werk," *Werke* (Königlich Preussische Akademie ed.) VII, 1, pp. 252 ff.

to the concept of the "classic." Nor is the fact that the painterly style customarily follows the linear and develops from
it, as is evident in the history of art, to be taken to imply the
argument that in this transformation we are dealing with an
instance of progress, of perfection. Instead, Wölfflin sees in
both styles merely divergent solutions to a specific problem,
each of which is equally justified aesthetically. *Within* each
of the two styles we are able to distinguish the perfect from
the imperfect, the inferior and mediocre from the superior.
But by no means do such distinctions admit of being extended to the two styles as wholes. Thus, according to
Wölfflin,

> The painterly mode is later and is not truly intelli-
> gible without the earlier, but is not superior in any
> absolute sense. The linear style developed values which
> the painterly style no longer possessed and no longer
> wanted to possess. They are two world views, differ-
> ently oriented in taste and in their interest in the
> world, and yet each is capable of giving a perfect pic-
> ture of visible things. . . . Always from a differently
> oriented interest in the world there comes to birth a
> different beauty.[12]

Thus far we have sought to lay bare the reasons which
justify and necessitate assigning culture-concepts to a place
of their own in contradistinction to historical concepts and
value concepts and to differentiate them in their logical
structure from both.

However, there remains still another question which till
now has not found solution. Is this autonomy of the concepts of form and style also independent of questions of

12. Wölfflin, pp. 18 and 27.

psychology? Is not the whole of culture—the development of language, art, and religion—comprehended within mental and spiritual processes? And do not all these processes *eo ipso* fall under the jurisdiction of psychology? Is there also a distinction [to be drawn] here? Can this conclusion be avoided or thrown into doubt? To be sure, there have always been eminent scholars who have doubted that it can, who, consequently, have drawn the [further] conclusion that there is no need to seek a science of principles for the humanities, that they lie ready and complete in psychology.

In the field of linguistics this thesis has been defended with particular clarity and emphasis by Herman Paul. Paul is, above all, an historian of language. He is not to be suspected of wishing to restrict the claim of the historical mode of inquiry to any particular mode. Instead, what he does insist on is that without reaching a settlement on questions of principle, without establishing the conditions of the historical process, no particular historical result whatsoever can be achieved. Hence, according to Paul, a science must always stand in support of the history of language, or of any other form of culture—[a science] which is itself "concerned with the universal conditions of the careers of historical, self-developing objects, and which seeks in all change the uniformly present factors, their nature and operation." These constant factors can only be found in psychology. Paul thinks of psychology as the psychology of individuals, not as *"Völkerpsychologie,"* as with Steinthal and Lazarus and later with Wundt. Thus the psychology of individuals is assigned the task of carrying forward to their solution the problems of principle in the theory of language. "Everything turns upon deducing the development of language from the reciprocal effects which individuals exercise upon each other."

The struggle between the "transcendental" and the "psychological" method in philosophy and in the general theory of science was at its bitterest when Herman Paul set forth this thesis in the beginning of his *Principles of the History of Language*. On the one side stood the Neo-Kantian schools, which insisted that the first and most important task of epistemological investigation is to distinguish between the *quid juris* and the *quid facti*. As empirical science, psychology is concerned with *questions of fact* which can never serve as norms for deciding *questions of value*. Today, *this* grudge between "logicism" and "psychologism," which for a long time determined the total character of philosophy, has to a certain extent receded into the background. After protracted battles, settlement has been reached on this issue; now it is scarcely ever seriously debated. Extremists among the psychologists had concluded that logic is the theory of the forms and laws of thought. As such, it is certainly a psychological discipline, since the processes of thought and learning exist only in the psyche.[13]

In his *Logische Untersuchungen* [Logical Inquiries] Husserl has exposed the paralogism which lay in this conclusion and, in a sense, has tracked it to its deepest hiding-place. He points out the radical and irresoluble difference between the form as "ideal unity of meaning" and the psychological experience, the "acts" of taking-as-true, of beliefs, and of judgments which refer themselves to this unity of meaning and have it as their object.[14] As a result, the danger of resolving logical and mathematical theory of forms into psychological states was averted.

13. Cf. Theodor Lipps, *Grundzüge der Logik* (Hamburg and Leipzig: L. Voss, 1893), pp. 1 ff.

14. Cf. Edmund Husserl, *Logische Untersuchungen* (Halle: M. Niemeyer, 1913–22), Vol. I, chap. 8.

To be sure, drawing this kind of dividing line [between act of thought and object of thought] appears at first glance to be far more difficult within the domain of the humanities. For we may well ask: Is there anywhere a fixed and enduring object in the case of language, art, myth, and religion? And does not all that we refer to in this manner reduce to simple acts of speech, artistic creation and enjoyment, mythical beliefs, and religious representations? Is there, in addition, an object of inquiry not completely enclosed within the sphere of these acts? But even a glance at the present state of the problem shows us that there is. Here, too, clarification has penetrated further and further.

In recent decades the psychology of language, the psychology of art, and the psychology of religion have grown ever more extensive. However, they no longer advance the claim of having superseded the *theory* of language, the *theory* of art, or the *theory* of religion, nor do they seek to make such theories superfluous. Here, too, the domain of a "theory of pure form" has taken shape with ever increasing clarity—a domain which employs other concepts than those of empirical psychology and which must be constructed by use of other methods. Karl Bühler's *Sprachtheorie* [Theory of Language] affords a striking example. It is all the more significant since Bühler came to the problems of language as a psychologist and, in the course of his research, never lost sight of this point of view. But, according to Bühler, the "nature" of language does not admit of being exhaustively rendered by either purely historical or purely psychological research. In the foreword to his work he insists that the question he is addressing to language is "What are you?," not "How did you get this way?" This is the old philosophic question of τί ἐστι. Here, with respect to method, "sematology" has laid claim to complete self-sufficiency. It is precisely as psychologist, and on the basis of psychological analyses, that Bühler consequently champions the thesis of the *ideality* of the objects of language. As he explains, "Language forms are, in Platonic terms, ideational objects; in terms of logic, they are classes of classes, like the numbers or objects of a higher formalization of scientific thought."[15] In this there lies the fact that, and the reasons why, "exhaustive classification of linguistics into series of 'idiographic sciences' is unsatisfactory and why a revision must be undertaken." According to Bühler the study of language will always turn out to be a kind of maverick so long as we insist on restricting it to an inquiry into historical facts or "reducing" it to physics and psychology conjointly.[16]

If we assume this position, all border-quarrels between philosophy of language and psychology of language cease. And perhaps we are already to the point where we can declare these quarrels to be unnecessary and outmoded. The particular problems have been clearly and precisely distinguished from one another. On the one hand, it is clear that the creation of a *theory* of language is not possible without constant reference to the results achieved in the history and psychology of language. Such a theory cannot be built up in the empty space of abstraction and speculation. But it is equally certain that empirical research in the field of linguistics, as in that of the psychology of language, must constantly presuppose concepts which are taken from the linguistic "theory of forms." If investigations are initiated to ascertain the sequence in which the various classes of words occur in the linguistic development of the child, or the

15. Karl Bühler, *Sprachtheorie* (Jena: Gustav Fischer, 1934), pp. 58 ff.
16. Bühler, p. 6.

phase in which the child passes from the "single-word sentence" to the "paratactical" sentence, and from this to the "hypotactical" sentence, it will be clear that, in the process, more or less fixed basic categories of the "theory of forms," of grammar, and of syntax have necessarily been assumed.[17] Elsewhere, too, it has been shown again and again that empirical research loses itself in pseudo-problems and insoluble antinomies, unless it is supported and constantly accompanied by careful conceptual reflection concerning what language *is*.

As we have indicated, Wölfflin has raised the complaint in his *Fundamental Concepts of Art History* that conceptual research in art history has not kept pace with factual research. We encounter similar complaints with increasing frequency today in the field of the psychology of language. As evidence of this we may cite an important article published recently by G. Révész under the title "Die menschlichen Kommunikationsformen und die sog. Tiersprache" [Human Forms of Communication and the so-called Language of Animals].[18] Révész begins with the reflection that countless "observations" which people have thought they had made concerning the "speech of animals," and many if not most of the experiments which have been initiated thus far in this area, have remained questionable or worthless because these researchers started without any precise *concept* of speech—because, at bottom, they did not know what they were asking or looking for. In this regard he calls for a radical change of method.

17. Cf., e.g., Clara and William Stern, *Die Kindersprache,* 2d ed. (Leipzig: J. A. Barth, 1920), chaps. XII–XV.
18. *Nederl. Akademie van Wetenschappen,* Vol. XLIII, No. 9 and 10, 1940, and XLIV, No. 1, 1941.

We must come to understand that the question as to the so-called speech of animals cannot be solved exclusively on the basis of the facts of animal psychology. Every impartial thesis and theory erected on the side of animal and developmental psychology which is subject to critical examination must eventually lead to the conviction that the problem [as it is] raised [merely] by demonstration of various forms of animal communication and by the achievements of various animal trainers (which themselves admit of the most contradictory interpretations) is not capable of being answered with logical rigor. Hence, we must endeavor to discover a logical and lawful starting point from which the facts of experience can find a natural and fruitful interpretation. This starting point is to be found in the definition of the concept of speech. . . . If we . . . take the pains to examine the so-called speech of animals from the standpoint of the philosophy and the psychology of language—in my opinion the only justified standpoint—we will not only give up the simple doctrine of animal speech but, at the same time, grasp in its full extent the meaningless statement of the problem in its present wording.

In my judgment these arguments upon which Révész bases his interpretation are of the utmost significance; however, we cannot pursue them further in this connection. I have adduced his statements at this point only to show how deeply the problem of language-structure is entangled in empirical research and how it cannot find its "sure way to science" until it gives due place to logical reflection. In the humanities, just as in science, the Kantian dictum concerning the relation of experience to reason holds good: "reason presupposes principles in her judgments and requires nature to answer her questions, but never allows herself to be led as if by nature's apron strings; otherwise fruitful observations depend on chance, following no previously projected plans, and are comprehended by no necessary law, which is indeed what reason seeks and demands."

Only after defining in this manner the concepts of form and style in the humanities, in contradistinction to other types of concepts, are we able to come to grips with a problem which is of decisive importance in applying these concepts to individual phenomena. We understand a science in its logical structure only when we have arrived at clarity as to the manner in which it achieves the *subsumption of the particular under the universal*. But in solving this problem we must be on our guard against a one-sided formalism. For there is no general schema which we may refer to or invoke. This *problem* is common to all the sciences; but its solution leads in many directions. Even within this very diversity a genuine and specific type of knowledge always expresses itself. To oppose "universal concepts" of natural science to "individual concepts" of historical science is clearly an unsatisfactory solution to the problem. According to its logical function, every concept seeks to be a "unity of the manifold," a relation between individual and universal. By isolating either of these factors one destroys the "synthesis" which every concept, as such, seeks to execute. "The particular," says Goethe, "is always more than a match for the universal; the universal always has to accommodate itself to the particular." But the manner of this "accommodating," this union of particulars through universals is not the same in all sciences. It is different when we compare the system of mathematical concepts and the empirical concepts of nature; and it is different when we contrast the latter to his-

torical concepts. Careful analyses of particulars are always
necessary in order to establish these differences.

This relationship appears in its simplest form when it
succeeds in expressing the universal as the *concept of a law*
from which the particular "instances" may be deduced.
Thus, for example, Kepler's formulas for the motions of the
planets or the formulas governing the periodic ebb and flow
of the tides "follow" from Newton's law of gravitation. Accordingly, all concepts of the empirical science of nature
strive in some particular way to attain this ideal, though not
all of them are able to realize it to this degree or in the same
manner. Always there persists the tendency of the empirical
coexistence of determinate [things] (which is all that observation exhibits at first) to change into other relations by virtue of intellectual manipulation—into relations of one
[state] *being conditioned* by another. It is this form of "subsumption" which succeeds better and more completely the
more the descriptive concepts of natural science are related
to theoretical concepts and become progressively transformed into the latter. If this were achieved, basically there
would no longer be any determination of particulars, any
empirical concepts. We would possess a fundamental determination from which all others would follow and be deducible in a fixed manner, as in purely mathematical concepts.
It is in this way that modern theoretical physics, for example, has succeeded in reducing all the particular "properties" of a given thing, all its determinations which are expressed in physical or chemical constants, to a common
source. This shows that the properties of an element, each
of which was initially discovered through empirical observation, are functions of a specific mass, that of their "atomic
weight"—that they cohere in a lawful manner to the "numerical order" of the element. Thus an empirically given
substance, a certain metal, can be subsumed under the con-

cept "gold" if, and only if, it exhibits the respective basic properties and hence all the other properties which admit of being deduced from it. Here no guessing is possible; for here "gold" *means* only what possesses a certain specific weight (itself strictly determinate quantitatively), a specific electrical conductivity, a specific coefficient of expansion, etc.

But if one expects something similar from the form and style concepts of the humanities, one is immediately disillusioned. They appear to be afflicted with a characteristic indeterminateness which they are unable to overcome. But here, too, it is possible to *coordinate* the particular with the universal; but it cannot be *subordinated* in the same manner. Here, again, I shall be content with illustrating the point at issue by means of a single concrete example. In his *Civilization of the Renaissance* Burckhardt gave a classic portrait of "the man of the Renaissance." It contains features that are familiar to everyone. The man of the Renaissance possesses definite characteristics, which clearly distinguish him from the "man of the Middle Ages." He is characterized by his delight in the senses, his turning to nature, his being rooted in "this side of existence," his openness in behalf of the world of forms, his individualism, his paganism, his amoralism. Empirical research set out to find this Burckhardtian "man of the Renaissance"; but it has not found him. No single historical individual can be cited who actually unites in himself all the traits that Burckhardt regards as elements constitutive of this image. In his *Studien zur Weltanschauung der Renaissance* Ernst Walser remarks that,

> If we attempt to view the life and thought of the leading personalities of the Quattrocento—of a Coluccio Salutati, a Poggio Bracciolini, a Leonardo Bruni, a

Lorenzo Valla, a Lorenzo Magnifico, or a Luigi Pulci—
in a purely inductive manner, the uniform result is
that for the particular persons being studied these
traits absolutely do *not* fit. If we attempt to conceive
what previously were only single coherent "characteristic traits," in strict correspondence with the careers
of these men, and, above all, with the broad stream of
the entire age, we find throughout a very different picture. As we bring together the results of inductive research, there gradually emerges a new image of the
Renaissance, no less a mixture of piety and impiety,
good and evil, other worldliness and earthiness, but infinitely more complicated. The life and striving of the
whole Renaissance cannot be derived from a *single*
principle, from individualism and sensualism, any
more than can *the much* lauded unity of the Middle
Ages.[19]

I agree completely with these words of Walser's. Anyone
who has ever been engaged in concrete research into the
history, literature, art, or philosophy of the Renaissance
will be able to confirm and document them amply from his
own experience. But does this confute Burckhardt's concept? Shall we regard it, in the logical sense, as a null class—
as a class containing no single member? That would be necessary only if we were concerned here with one of those
generic concepts arrived at through empirical comparison
of particular cases, through what we commonly call "induc-
tion." Judged by *this* standard, Burckhardt's concept cannot measure up.

19. Ernst Walser, *Studien zur Weltanschauung der Renaissance,*
now in *Gesammelte Studien zur Geistesgeschichte der Renaissance*
(Basel: Benno Schwabe & Co., 1932), p. 102.

But it is just this *presupposition* that needs logical revision. Burckhardt could not have given his image of "the man of the Renaissance" without relying upon an immense amount of factual material in support of it. The wealth of this material and its trustworthiness astonish us again and again as we study his work. But the kind of "conspectus" he executes, the historical synthesis he gives, is wholly different in kind from that of empirically acquired concepts of nature. If we wish to speak of "abstraction" here it is that we are dealing with that process which Husserl characterized as *"ideirende* abstraction." That the result of such an *"ideirende* abstraction" could ever be brought to coincide with any concrete case—this can neither be expected nor demanded. And "subsumption" can never be taken here in the same sense in which we subsume a body given here and now, i.e., a piece of metal, under the concept "gold," after finding that it fulfills all the conditions of gold known to us. When we characterize Leonardo da Vinci and Aretino, Marsiglio Ficino and Machiavelli, Michelangelo and Cesare Borgia as "men of the Renaissance," we do not mean to say that there is to be found in them a definite and inherently fixed distinguishing trait in which they all agree. We perceive them to be not only completely different, but even opposed. What we are asserting of them is that in spite of this opposition, perhaps just because of it, they stand to each other in a specific ideal connection: each in his own way is contributing to the making of what we call the "spirit" of the Renaissance or the civilization of the Renaissance.

What we are trying to give expression to here is a unity of *direction,* not a unity of *actualization.* The particular individuals *belong together,* not because they are alike or resemble each other, but because they are *cooperating in* a *common task,* which, in contrast to the Middle Ages, we perceive to be new and to be the distinctive "meaning" of the Renaissance. All genuine concepts of style in the humanities reduce, when analyzed more precisely, to such conceptions of meaning. The artistic style of an epoch cannot be determined unless we gather into a unity all its divergent and often patently disparate artistic expressions, unless, to use Riegl's expression, we understand them as manifestations of a specific "artistic will."[20] Such expressions do indeed *characterize* but they do not *determine;* for the particulars which they comprehend cannot be deduced from them.

But it is equally incorrect to infer from this that we have only intuitive description here, and not conceptual characterization; we are dealing with a distinctive manner and direction of characterization, with a logico-intellectual activity which is *sui generis.*

At this point we pause in order, first of all, to look once again at earlier observations. The result of our analysis of concepts of style assumes its full significance only when we compare it with the result of our phenomenological analysis. What emerges is not only a parallelism, but a genuine interdependence. The distinction between concepts of form and style, on the one hand, and thing-concepts, on the other hand, reveals that same opposition which we encountered earlier in [analyzing] the structure of perception. It is, so to speak, the logical translation of a definite *opposition in orientation,* which as such is not encountered solely in the domain of concepts, but whose roots run deep into the subsoil of perception. Here conception expresses "discursively" what perception apprehends in the form of a purely "intui-

20. Alois Riegl, *Stilfragen* (Berlin: R. C. Schmidt & Co., 1893), and *Spätrömische Kunstindustrie* (Vienna: Austrian Press, 1927).

tive" knowledge [*Erkenntnis*]. The "reality" which we apprehend in perception and direct intuition presents itself to us as a whole in which there are no abrupt separations. And yet, it is both "one and twofold"; for, on the one hand, we apprehend it as thing-like and, on the other hand, as "personal."

One of the primary tasks of any critique of knowledge consists in clarifying the logical constitution of each of these two fundamental forms of experience. For the world of things, for that which we call "physical" reality, Kant has answered this question tersely and suggestively. What is coherent with the material conditions of experience, with sensation, in accordance with universal laws, is real. Physical reality by no means derives from sensation. It is not bound to the mere here-and-now. It places the here-and-now within a context that is universal and systematic; it inserts it into the system of space and time. All conceptual manipulation by science of the "material" of sensation serves ultimately this *one* goal. In the course of the development of science this work has become ever richer and more abundant; it continues to become more subtle as logical analysis persists in following out its course in detail. Nevertheless, insofar as a schematic simplification is allowable, it admits, in essence, of being reduced to two fundamental factors.

Property-constants and *law-constants* are the two essential features of the physical world. When we speak of a "cosmos," what we mean is that we can, in some sense, fix the Heraclitean flux of becoming, that we are able to single out enduring distinctions within it. It is not only where philosophical and scientific theory looms forth with its independent claims that this transition occurs; this tendency toward "fixing" already belongs to perception: without it we could never attain perception of "things." Even perception—even sight, hearing, and touch—realize that first step which all formation of concepts must presuppose and refer to. For even here there is enacted that process of reading-off, by virtue of which we distinguish the "real" color of an object from its apparent color and its true size from its apparent size. The modern psychology and physiology of sense perception have moved this process into the center of attention and pursued it from all sides. The problem of the constants of perception constitutes one of its weightiest and epistemologically most fruitful problems. For, from this point on, a bridge can be built joining perceptual cognition with the remotest construction of concepts in exact science—in particular, with mathematical group theory.

Science is distinguished here from perception—in a highly significant way, to be sure—only by the fact that it requires a strict *determination* where perception contents itself with a mere *estimate*.[21] To this end, it demands the development of newer and more appropriate methods. It determines the "essence" of things entirely in numerical concepts and in the physical and chemical constants which are characteristic of every class of objects as things. It establishes this [class] connection by the fact that it unites these constants through fixed functional relationships, through equations expressing the dependence of one magnitude upon another. Only in this way have we attained the sure scaffolding to "objective" reality; it is in this way that the one common [conceptual] world of things is constitutively realized. But this result is necessarily bought at a sacrifice. This thing-world is inherently soulless. All that harks back,

21. For more details see my article, "Le concept de groupe et la théorie de la perception," *Journal de Psychologie* (1938), 368–414. [English trans., "The Concept of Group and the Theory of Perception," *Philosophy and Phenomenological Research*, V (1944), 1–35.]

in any way, to the "personal" experience of the ego is not only suppressed; it is removed and extinguished.

As a result, human culture can find no place of its own in *this* scheme of nature. Still, culture is *also* an "inter-subjective world," a world which does not have its being in "me," but which is necessarily accessible to all subjects, and in which they necessarily participate. But this *partici-pation* is radically different from that in the physical world. Instead of relating themselves to the selfsame spacio-temporal cosmos of things, they find and relate themselves within the medium of the various worlds of form out of which culture comes into being. Here, too, perception must take that first and decisive step—here, too, it is the passage from the "I" to the "you." But passive experience of ex-pression is as inadequate here as mere feeling, simple "impression," is for knowledge of objects. This genuine "synthesis" is first realized in that active exchange which we encounter directly in every verbal [act of imparting] "information."

The constancy required for this is not that of properties or laws, but of meanings. The more culture develops, and the more the particular areas into which it unfolds, the more richly and multifariously does this world of meanings shape itself. We *live within* the words of language, the shapes of poetry and plastic art, the structure of music, the framework of religious representation and religious be-liefs. And it is only within these [media] that we "know" each other. This intuitive knowledge does not yet have the character of "science." We understand one another in speech without first requiring linguistics or grammar; and "natural" artistic feeling does not require art history or stylistics. But this "natural" understanding soon comes to its limits. We can no more reach the depths of culture with the elements of intuition than simple sense perception can penetrate the depths of cosmic space. In both cases, only what is near is intelligible; the remote loses itself in mist and darkness. It is at these limits that the efforts and achievements of science intervene.

When it raises itself to the knowledge of universal laws for which there is no difference between the near and the distant, natural science becomes master of the distant. It begins with observations which can be made in our immediate environment. It begins with rules which it discovers concerning the free fall of bodies. But it expands this discovery into the universal law of gravitation, the scope of which is the whole of cosmic space.

This form of universality is closed to the science of culture. It cannot renounce anthropomorphism and anthropocentrism. Its subject matter is not the world as such but a particular region of it, which appears infinitesimal from a purely spacial standpoint. But if it does stop short with the human world, and hence remain within the confines of strictly earthly existence, it strives, accordingly, to completely penetrate this, its proper sphere. Its goal is not the universality of laws; but neither is it the individuality of facts and phenomena. In contrast to both, it sets up an ideal of knowledge of its own. What it seeks to realize is the *totality* of the *forms* in which human life is realized. These forms are endlessly divergent and, yet, they are not without unified structure. For in the end it is "one and the same" human nature which meets us again and again in a thousand manifestations and in a thousand masks in the development of culture. We do not become aware of this identity through watching, weighing, and measuring. Nor do we come upon it through psychological inductions. It can only be *demonstrated within* the *act* [of its realization]. A culture is accessible to us only if we are actively involved in it; but this involvement is not bound to the immediate present. Here the distinctions of time, distinctions of earlier and later, are relative, just as spacial distinctions, distinctions of here and there, are as rendered by physics and astronomy.

Each of these renderings entails a highly subtle and complex conceptual mediation. In the one case, the grasp is executed by means of thing- and law-concepts; in the other case, it is achieved through concepts of form and style. Historical knowledge enters as an indispensable factor in this process; but it is the means, not the end in itself.

The task of history does not consist merely in making us *acquainted with* past existence and life, but in teaching us how *to interpret* its meaning. All mere knowledge of the past would remain for us a "lifeless picture" if no other powers were involved than those of reproductive memory. What memory preserves of facts and events only becomes historical recollection by means of the fact that we are able to relate it to our inner experience and transform it into such experience. Ranke has remarked that the genuine task of the historian is to describe "as it actually was." But even if we accept this statement, it is still true that "what has been," acquires a new meaning when placed in the perspective of history. History is not simply chronology, and historical time is not objective physical time. The past is not gone for the historian in the same sense as for the natural scientist; it possesses and retains a present peculiar to itself. The geologist may give us information concerning a past shape of the earth; the paleontologist tells us of extinct organic forms. All this "existed" once and cannot be renewed in its existence and true character.

However, history never attempts to set before us *mere*

past existence; it seeks to teach us to *understand* life in the past. The content of this life it cannot renew; still, it endeavors to preserve its pure form. The wealth of different concepts of form and style which have found expression in the humanities [*Kulturwissenschaften*], in the final analysis, are engaged in a single task: only through them is the rebirth, the "palingenesis," of culture possible. What is actually preserved for us from the past are specific historical monuments—"monuments" in word and writing, in picture and in bronze. This first becomes history for us when in these monuments we see symbols, through which we not only recognize specific forms of life, but by virtue of which we are able to restore them for ourselves.

2

Any theory which defends the logical autonomy of concepts of style finds itself faced above all with the attacks raised against this autonomy by the naturalism of the nineteenth century. The most acute and most consistent attempt to contest every feature of the concepts of style was undertaken by Hippolyte Taine. The attempt is all the more convincing because Taine does not stop with mere theory, but immediately proceeds to translate it into fact. In his *Philosophie de l'Art* and in his *History of English Literature* he has carried out his thesis in a brilliant manner. Within a single subject matter, comprehending nearly all great epochs in the history of art and literature, he was determined to prove that the sciences of literature and art can be handled in a truly scientific manner only if they renounce any claim to autonomous status. Instead of seeking in any way to differentiate themselves from natural science, they must be completely reduced to it. For all scientific knowing is causal knowing. And just as there certainly are not two orders of causation—one "spiritual" the other "natural"—so, too, there cannot be a "science of the spiritual" in addition to "the science of nature." Taine's explanation is as follows:

> The modern method which I seek to pursue and which is now beginning to become dominant in all the humanities *(sciences morales)* consists in regarding human works, and art works in particular, as facts and products whose properties must be ascertained and whose causes must be fathomed—nothing else. Science neither repudiates nor distorts; it ascertains and explains. . . . This science [of culture] proceeds like botany, which studies the orange tree and the laurel, the fir and the birch with equal interest. It is in itself a kind of botany, with reference not to plants but to the works of man. In this respect it follows the same tendency which is bringing the humanities closer to the natural sciences and which assures to the former the same certainty and progress by providing it with the principles and frames of reference of the latter.[22]

It is well known how Taine sought to solve the problem he set for himself here. If the reduction of cultural science to natural science is to succeed, then, above all, an attempt must be made to gain mastery of the puzzling plurality of cultural events. At first glance, in language, in art, in religion, in social and political life, we discern nothing but a variegated multiplicity, a continuous exchange of partic-

22. Hippolyte Taine, *The Philosophy of Art,* trans. and rev. by the author (New York: Bailliere Brothers, 1865), Part I, chap. 1, par. 1.

ular forms. No one is the same as another and none ever returns again in the same manner. But we must not allow
ourselves to become confused or blinded by this colorful
abundance. Here, too, knowledge must pursue the course
taken by natural science. It must reduce the facts to laws
and the laws to principles. Then the appearance of diversity
vanishes; there emerges a uniformity and simplicity which
can vie with that of exact science. In mental as in physical
events we meet with specific and constant factors, with irreducible forces which always operate in the same way.
"There is a single series of the more extensive and universal
causes; the universal structure of things and the great pro-
gression of events are its work. Religions, philosophy, poetry, industry and technology, the forms of society and
family are ultimately nothing but the imprint given to
events by this universal system of causation."[23]

Our concern here is not with the extent to which Taine
has given factual evidence for his basic thesis of strict determinism.[24] We are dealing merely with the logical aspect
of the problem, with the concepts which Taine takes as
basic, and with the methods which he brings to bear in his
interpretation of cultural phenomena. If he is serious about
remaining true to his first principle, he is obliged to develop his "concepts of culture" from his "concepts of nature." He must show how the one ties itself directly to the
other and proceeds from it. And just this was evidently the
goal which he believed he had reached when he set forth

23. Taine, "Introduction" to *History of English Literature*, trans.
Henri van Laun (New York: The Colonial Press, 1900).

24. On this problem consult my article "Naturalistische und hu-
manistische Begründung der Kulturphilosophie," *Göteborg Kungl.
Vetenskaps-och Vitterhets-Samhälles Handlingar.* 5e foljden, Ser. A,
Band 7, No. 3 (1939).

his famous triad as scientific first principles of culture. These ultimate grounds of explanation—the concepts of *race, milieu,* and *moment*—do not, in the least, appear to go beyond the sphere which we are able to discern by using the instruments of pure natural science. And yet, they contain in germ all that we demand in the derivation of the most complex phenomena of cultural science. They fulfill the double condition of presenting a completely simple and incontestable state of affairs, which is, at the same time, capable of extraordinary variation, which recurs as homogeneous throughout the most diverse instances of its application. One must continually marvel at the art with which Taine, in his concrete portraits of individuals, has filled them with intuitive vigor and given life to the inflexible scheme which he takes as fundamental.

However, if one inquires into how this accomplishment was achieved, a very curious and methodologically intricate state of affairs emerges. For without notice we are continually led to a point at which Taine's mode of explanation reverts dialectically, so to speak, to its own opposite. We may clarify this by means of one specific example—his treatment of Netherlandic painting in the seventeenth century. True to his maxim, Taine begins here with the "universal" causes. Holland is the land of alluvial deposits; it has been built up from the deposits which the great rivers carry and discharge at their mouths. The basic character of the land and its inhabitants is given in this one feature. We see before us the climate and atmosphere in which the Netherlandic man has grown up and we realize how this atmosphere necessarily determined all his physical, moral, and intellectual characteristics. Netherlandic art is nothing but the natural and necessary imprint and manifestation of just these traits.

In this way speculative-idealistic aesthetics admits of being [dialectically] opposed to a materialistic, and naturalistic aesthetics—the "aesthetics from above" or the "aesthetics from below." Intellectual rigor requires that we proceed step by step at just this point. Continuity in the succession of causes must not be broken. [According to Taine's thesis,] there must nowhere be a sudden leap from the "physical" to the "spiritual." We must proceed from the inorganic world to the organic, from physics to biology, and from this to the specifically anthropological. But with this we have reached our goal; for, as soon as we have come to know man for what he is, we have also understood his achievements.

This program sounds promising in every respect. But has Taine really carried it through? Has he advanced continuously from physics to botany and zoology, to anatomy and physiology, ending with psychology and characterology, thus finally giving explanation to the individual phenomena of culture? If we examine the matter more closely, we find that this is by no means the case. Taine begins by speaking the language of the natural scientist; but we perceive that he is not at home in this language. The further he proceeds and the closer he comes to the genuine and concrete problems, the more he finds himself obliged to think and speak in a language whose concepts are different [in kind]. He sets out from the concepts and starting points of natural science, but in the course of his work both undergo a genuine *change of meaning*. When Taine speaks of the Greek, Italian, or Netherlandic landscape, he must, if he is determined to remain true to his method, describe this landscape in terms of its "physical" features, as geology or geography. And there is no lack of statements to this effect, as we have seen. But presently we meet with a wholly different characteristic, which, in contrast to the physical, we may call a "physiognomic" characteristic. Now the landscape is gloomy or cheerful, severe or delightful, gentle or sublime. Clearly, none of these characteristics admits of being determined by means of scientific observation of nature. Instead they are pure expression-characters. And only by virtue of these characters does Taine succeed in building the bridge which leads him to the world of Greek, Italian, and Netherlandic art.

The facts of the case emerge with particular clarity as soon as Taine approaches the genuinely anthropological problem. His thesis requires that he relate each great epoch of culture to a determinate human type and deduce it from that origin. Accordingly, he must show that, by virtue of his race and the particular physical determinations which follow from it, a Greek must necessarily become the creator of the Homeric poems and the Parthenon frieze, an Englishman the creator of Elizabethan dramas, an Italian the creator of the *Divine Comedy* and the Sistine Chapel. But Taine has avoided all such problematic constructions.

Here, too, he has recourse to a brief attempt to speak the conceptual language of natural science but, then, suddenly, he is bent on speaking the language of expression. Instead of basing himself on anatomy or physiology, he entrusts himself to a completely different mode of knowledge. From the standpoint of logic, this might appear to be a regression and a contradiction; but from the standpoint of his own problem, it is a decided gain. For only thus does his dry logical schema—the schema of race, milieu, and moment—achieve color and life. At this point, personality not only claims its rightful place; it is declared to be the very focus of all cultural historical study. "Rien n'existe que par l'individu; c'est l'individu lui-même qu'il faut connaître."

Only through him does the quality of the artistic, social, and religious life of an age reveal itself. "A dogma is nothing in itself; to understand it, observe the men who made it; study this or that portrait of the sixteenth century—the hard and energetic face of an archbishop or an English martyr. We first glimpse real history when the historian succeeds, in addition, in looking beyond the passage of time to the living human beings . . . with their voices and faces, their gestures and clothing."[25]

But whence comes this concrete knowledge of men, which, according to Taine, constitutes the alpha and omega of cultural history? What we demand is that Taine forthrightly give up his central thesis that, since all culture is the work of human beings, once we have insight into the nature of human beings, everything else about it is completely determinate. Kant, who was one of the most radical champions of the idea of freedom in the history of philosophy, has, nevertheless, said that if we were to know completely the empirical character of a human being, we could predict all his future actions with the same certainty as astronomy predicts a solar or lunar eclipse. If we turn from individuals to universals, we may then state that as soon as we once know the character of Netherlanders of the seventeenth century, everything else [pertaining to them] is given. From this knowledge we can deduce all [their] cultural configurations: we comprehend why the Netherlands at this time experienced a transformation in its political and religious life, a great economic revival, an awakening in freedom of thought, and a flowering of scientific and artistic life.

However, the most complete insight into this actual nexus

25. Taine, *History of English Literature,* Introduction.

of cause and effect would not answer our *logically* prior question. For logic does not ask for the *actual bases of events,* but for the *bases of knowledge.* For it, the genuinely primary question is: to what mode of knowledge do we owe our understanding of man as the bearer and creator of culture? And here we see in Taine himself, and in the very midst of his own presentation, a highly remarkable turn of events. Taine has not drawn his knowledge of the Greeks of classical times, of the Englishmen of Renaissance, and of the Netherlanders of the seventeenth century, merely from historical archives. He is equally far from drawing his support for this from scientific observations and arguments concerning nature, or from what he is able to learn from the psychology laboratory. For, as he himself insists, in all this we have only separate features—we are unable to form *any total image* of man. But what is the basis for this total image which Taine presents to us with such intuitiveness, and to which he refers so often as if to the actual ground of explanation?

In order not to arouse the suspicion that we are introducing anything into Taine's theory, we shall answer this question with his own words. How is it, he asks himself, that we have such exact knowledge of the Flemish of the seventeenth century that we all but have the impression of having lived among them? What is it that makes them immediately familiar to us? And Taine's answer is that the first to see these Flemish as we see them today was none other than Rubens and that it was by him that their image has been indelibly stamped on us. But at this point Taine goes even a step further. He tells us, not only that Rubens *discovered* this typical image of the Flemish and captured it in his art, but that he *created* it. He could not have taken it from direct observation of nature and he could not have achieved it by

simple empirical ["inductive"] comparison. For no "actual"
Netherlander possessed what Rubens intended and has
given us.

"Go to Flanders," Taine tells us,

> and observe there the human types in their moments
> of joy and merry making, such as the feasts at Ghent or
> Antwerp. You will see happy people eating much and
> drinking even more, smoking their pipes in complete
> serenity, phlegmatic, understanding, and relaxed, with
> massive irregular features similar to those of Teniers.
> As for the splendid brutes of Rubens' *Kermesse,* you
> will find nothing resembling them. Rubens must have
> found them elsewhere. The model for them lay in him-
> self. He felt in himself the poetry of this gross volup-
> tuous living, the exuberant, uninhibited and shameless
> sensuality, the animal pleasure which unfolded in gi-
> gantic proportions. In order to express all this . . . he
> has painted into his *Kermesse* the most astonishing tri-
> umph of human bestiality a painter's brush ever pre-
> sented. If the artist alters the proportions of the parts
> of the human body in rendering it, he continually al-
> ters it with one and the same interpretation and with a
> fixed intention. What he seeks in this is to make visible
> an essential character (*caractère essentiel*) of the object
> and the dominant idea (*idée principale*) which he has
> of it. But note the word! This character is what the phi-
> losopher calls the essence of things (*l'essence des
> choses*). *But* what *we* intend by it is description—the
> avoidance of a *terminus technicus* essence. Instead, we
> will simply state that the task of art is to manifest the
> basic character of an object, some salient noteworthy
> quality, some important point of view, one of its prin-

cipal features. (L'art a pour but de manifester le caractère capital, quelque qualité saillante et notable, un
point de vue important, une manière d'être principale
de l'objet.)[26]

All these paraphrastic statements concerning the object of
art remain so many riddles when we reflect on the starting
point of Taine's theory. For how, indeed, are we to determine what the "essence" of a specific intuitive object, or
its "salient character," its principal quality, consists in?
Clearly, direct empirical observation forsakes us here. For
all the attributes which it affords us—seen from *its* standpoint [as object]— lie on an even plane. No single attribute
possesses an essence or value advantage over any other. It is
equally clear that statistical methods are of no avail here
either. The image of the Netherlanders that Rubens gives
in his paintings is, indeed, according to Taine himself, by
no means seen as a mere average composited from hundreds
of separate observations. It does not originate from direct
observation of nature and was not discovered by this latter
means. It originates in the soul of the artist; for only this
was capable of distinguishing in this way the "essential"
from the "non-essential," the determinate and dominating
from the accidental.

In nature the character is merely prevalent; the concern in art is to make it dominate. (Dans la nature le
caractère n'est que dominant; il s'agit, dans l'art, de
le rendre dominateur.) This character shapes the real

26. Hippolyte Taine, *Philosophie de l'art,* Prem. partie Chap. I,
Sec. V. Trans. John Durand as *Lectures on Art* (New York: Henry
Holt and Company, 1875), pp. 62–65.

object; but it does not shape it completely. In its effectiveness it is limited by the interaction of other causes.
It is unable to stamp itself upon the object in a perfectly clear and visible imprint. Man fills this gap—
and in filling it he discovers art.[27]

As he wrote these sentences, Taine did not believe that he
had, in any way, broken the circle of the strictly naturalistic
theory. Yet it is perfectly obvious that these statements
could appear in any "idealistic" aesthetic and that Taine
here attributes to such an aesthetic all that he seemed initially to be arguing against.[28] With this, art possesses one of
its authentic, creative *functions* and, at the same time, it distinguishes the essential from the nonessential, the necessary
from the accidental. It does not simply surrender itself to
empirical observation and the mass of individual cases, but
"discriminates, selects, and corrects."

This knowledge of the "essential" which we encounter
here we do not owe to the inductive method of natural science. Instead, the necessary means to this knowledge is a
Homer or a Pindar, a Michelangelo or a Raphael, a Dante or
a Shakespeare. It is the intuition of the great artist which
has created for us, and established in its basic features, our
image of the Greeks of classical antiquity, of the Italians
and the English of the Renaissance.

Here it is evident that, in order to arrive at a specific and
concrete result, Taine's thinking is obliged to move in a

27. *Ibid.*
28. This is all the more glaring in that, in principle, Taine sub-
scribes completely to the "theory of imitation." He is determined to
explain, not only poetry, painting and sculpture, but even architecture and music as "imitating arts," with the result, of course, that he is
forced to resort to an extremely artificial and forced construction.

peculiar circular motion. Taine sought to explain and deduce the world of art forms from the world of physical forces. But he was obliged to reintroduce art forms under another label. For only in this way was he able to inject into the "flowing but ever recurring succession" of natural phenomena and natural causes those specific distinctions which his interpretation necessarily demanded.

Taine's first move in this direction was decisive for all that followed. When this occurred, the armor of the strictly naturalistic method was already pierced. For now, unincumbered by any kind of dogmatic presuppositions, Taine is free to abandon himself once again to "naive" intuition —and this he does to the fullest. Geology and geography, botany and zoology, anatomy and physiology are gradually forgotten. When Taine depicts the nature of Holland, he surrenders himself without reserve to what the Dutch landscape painters have taught him about it. And when he speaks of the Greek race, he relies, not on anthropological observations and measurements, but on Greek sculpture— on what Phidias and Praxiteles have taught him.

It is no wonder that this study allows itself to be reversed, that art admits of being "deduced" from nature; for an image of nature has been formed which derived its fixed and fundamental features, as well as its verification, from art.

The difficulty that faces us here points to a completely universal problem, which, sooner or later, will make itself felt in any employment of principles in the humanities. The object of *nature* appears to lie immediately before our eyes. To be sure, keener epistemological analysis teaches us [to know better] whenever more numerous and more complicated concepts are required in order to define this object, in order to determine the characteristics of the "objects" of physics, chemistry, and biology. But this determination perfects itself in a certain uniform direction: we go to and from the object, as it were, in order to learn to know it ever more exactly.

But the cultural object requires a different [kind of] observation; for it lies in back of us, so to speak. Indeed, at first sight it appears to be more familiar and more accessible than any other object. For what can man comprehend sooner and more completely—as Vico has remarked—than what he has himself created? But even here there emerges a limit to knowledge which is not easy to overcome. For the *reflexive* process of conception is opposed in tendency to the *productive* process; both cannot be accomplished at one and the same time. Culture is forever creating new linguistic, artistic, and religious symbols in an uninterrupted stream. But science and philosophy must analyze this language of symbols into its elements in order to make it intelligible. They must treat analytically what was produced synthetically. A ceaseless motion and counter-motion prevails here. In Kant's expression, natural science teaches us "to break up *appearances* into their syllables in order that we may read them off as *experiences*"; the science of culture teaches us to *interpret symbols* in order to decipher their *latent meaning,* to make visible again the life from which they originally came into being.

CHAPTER 4

The Problem of Form
and the Problem of Causality

THE CONCEPT OF FORM and the concept of cause constitute the two poles upon which our understanding of the world rotates. They are both indispensable if our thought is to arrive at the establishment of a fixed world order. The initial step necessarily consists in articulating the manifold of being which we encounter in direct perception, subdividing it according to specific shapes, classes, and types. But, next to the question of being, there stands the question of becoming—equally original and equally valid. Not only the "what" of the world but also the "whence" is to be understood.

Myth is already familiar with both questions. All that it comprehends—world as well as gods—it beholds under this double aspect. Even the Gods have their being and their becoming—mythical theology accompanies mythical theogony. Philosophical thought stands opposed to myth and constitutes a novel and unique mode of our knowledge of the world. But, from the first, we find even in it the same cleavage, which soon deepens into a conscious opposition. The concepts of form and cause had no sooner found their first rigorous interpretation, than they also began to oppose each other. The struggle that ensued between them fills the entire history of Greek philosophy and gives it its peculiar stamp. Here "structural thinking" and "causal thinking" do not diverge; instead, they actively oppose each other as inimical opposites. The Ionian philosophers of nature, Empedocles, Anaxagoras, and the atomists inquire into the cause of becoming. *Rerum cognoscere causas*—this constitutes the true goal of their thought and investigation. Democritus has said that he would rather discover a single "aitiology" than be ruler over the whole of the Persian Empire. But next to the "physiologists," who seek the ground of coming-to-be and development, there stands another group of thinkers, who deny that there is birth and genesis, and who consequently are obliged to explain the question of its origin as self-deception. In Plato's *Theaetetus,* Parmenides is described as their father and progenitor.[1] Plato himself has portrayed with classical poignancy and vividness how the mighty transition, which led him from becoming to being, from the problem of cause to the problem of form, came full circle in his own intellectual development. He tells us in the *Phaedo* how eagerly he had gotten hold of a copy of the book by Anaxagoras, just because *"nous"* (reason) was advanced there as the first principle of the universe. But he soon put it down in disillusionment; for, instead of the sought-for principle of reason, he found only another mechanical cause. He was forced to make a "second voyage"—and it was this one which first carried him to the shores of the world of ideas.

The Aristotelian system promises a different reconciliation of opposites. In opposition to the philosophers of pure form, Plato and the Eleatics, Aristotle is determined to re-

1. Plato, *Theaetetus,* 183 E.

store Becoming to its rightful place; for he is convinced that only in this way can philosophy be transformed from a mere theory of concepts into a theory of the actual. But on the other hand, like Plato, he sees the knowledge of form as the proper goal of any scientific explanation of the world. Form and matter, being and becoming, must be correlative if such an explanation is to be possible. The peculiarly Aristotelian concept of form-cause originates in this correlativity. The material cause which the atomists had seized upon in their eagerness for "aitiology" is incapable of answering the question as to the why of becoming. For it lacks what [the concept of] becoming first makes intelligible, what it welds into a whole. A true whole cannot originate in a [merely] mechanical aggregation of parts. Genuine wholeness emerges only where all parts are dominated by a single purpose and strive to realize it. Actuality ["*Wirklichkeit*"] is accessible to scientific conceptualization and philosophic understanding just because of the fact that it exhibits this structure, because what exists is organic being and organic coming-to-be. Here the form-principle and the causal principle coincide for both are united in the telic principle. Αἰτία, εἶδος, and τέλος are only three different expressions for one and the same state of affairs.

Thus, the Aristotelian philosophy appears to have succeeded not only in reconciling the concepts of form and cause but also in enabling reduction of the one to the other. Considerations of form, cause, and end can be deduced from a still higher principle. Here lay one of the greatest achievements of the Aristotelian system. For there now emerges a most remarkable unity and completeness in the understanding of the world. Physics and biology, cosmology and theology, ethics and metaphysics were related to a single universal cause. They all found their unity in God as the unmoved mover. So long as *this* achievement remained un-contested, Aristotelianism could not be seriously shaken. Because of it Aristotelianism has maintained its dominance over the centuries.

But by the fourteenth century there appear increasing indications that this domination is no longer regarded as beyond dispute. William of Ockham and his followers pro-ceed to construct a new view of nature; they set forth a theory of motion which in many ways contradicts the first principles of Aristotelian physics. Moreover, in the first cen-turies of the Renaissance a continuous quarrel broke out between Aristotelians and Platonists. But meanwhile, the collapse of Aristotelianism came about neither as a [direct] result of dialectic debate nor of empirical research. Aris-totle remained invincible so long as his fundamental con-cept, the concept of form-cause, was able to maintain its key position. Only when the attacks were directed against this point was it possible to unhinge the system.

This occurred when the mathematical science of nature emerged with its claims and then only when it had not only actually achieved its ideal of knowledge but had subse-quently sought to ground it philosophically. With this the concept of causality undergoes a transformation which ap-pears both to allow and to demand its complete separation from the concept of form. For mathematics—which with Plato still remained wholly within the sphere of being—had now moved into the sphere of becoming. With its mathematical form the dynamics of Galileo opened up the realm of becoming and made it accessible to strict concep-tual knowledge. Accordingly, all claims of the Aristotelian concept of form-cause were denounced as worthless. Only the mathematical cause is a *causa vera*. The Aristotelian forms are nothing but "dark qualities," which must be banned from [empirical] research. With this there begins that triumph of mathematical thought and "mechanical causality" by virtue of which they come to comprehend each other within a single sphere. Descartes makes use of Harvey's discovery of the circulation of blood to demonstrate in it the necessity of the mechanical method of explanation. Already Hobbes holds to a *definition* of philosophy from which not only the supremacy but even the universal validity of the concept of causality is the consequence. According to him, philosophy is "knowledge of effects, or phenomena, from their causes, or principles." Consequently, anything ungenerated, anything eternal, such as the Peripatetic-Scholastic forms, can never be an object of knowledge; such a thing is but an empty word, which must be eliminated from philosophy and science.

But, with this rejection of concepts of form, the gulf between natural science and the humanities becomes evident once again. For the latter cannot do without concepts of form without ceasing to exist. In linguistics, art criticism, and the study of religion, the very things we are trying to understand are specific "forms," forms which we must understand purely in themselves before we can possibly attempt to derive them from their causes. The claims of the concept of causality are by no means thrown into doubt or distorted as a result. They are restricted, inasmuch as they are confronted by another claimant to knowledge. The upshot is that contention and clash of method break out anew. This bitterness reaches its high point in the philosophies of the nineteenth century.

At last, in the world view of "historical materialism," it becomes evident that the ultimate decision has been reached, the final judgment has found expression. Historical materialism had advanced to a new and crucial layer of events, which instantly reduced cultural creations to a strictly causal treatment and seemed, consequently, to be the first to make them truly intelligible. For it, cultural forms do not exist in their own right; they are merely the "superstructure," which rests on another and deeper base. When we reach this base, when we acknowledge economic phenomena and tendencies as the actual driving forces of all events, it becomes evident that all dualism is removed and unity restored.

When the humanities resolved to dispute this decree, they found themselves faced with a difficult task. For what could they set over against mathematics, mechanics, physics, and chemistry? Was it not inevitable that any such attacks upon the armored car of the mathematical-scientific method would merely bounce off? Does not the logic of clear and distinct ideas undeniably stand on the side of the latter, and isn't the former compelled to support itself upon indeterminate emotional demands, upon mere "inclinations"? Actually the humanities had scarcely begun to do battle when unexpected aid came to them from another quarter. So long as natural science stood firmly upon the basis of the "mechanical world view," the absolute sway of this world view was hardly to be broken. But it was just here that that remarkable development occurred which led to an inner crisis and finally to a "revolution in our mode of thinking" within the field of the [exact] science of nature itself. Since the beginning of the twentieth century, it has made its appearance with growing clarity in all areas. In quick succession, it gains possession of physics, biology, and psychology.

This turn of events also sets out from the *concept of form;* but it no longer understands it in its old Aristotelian meaning. Briefly, the difference is that the factor of *whole-*

ness in the Aristotelian conception of form is retained, but not that of *purposiveness*. Aristotle had proceeded anthropomorphically. He had set out from the purposive action of human beings and had read this into the whole of nature. When the architect builds a house, the whole is prior to the individual parts; for the plan and blueprint, the representation of the shape of the house, precedes the execution of the particulars. From this, Aristotle draws the conclusion that where this kind of priority can be established, a purposive operation must always be presupposed. And the premise for this conclusion he finds universally substantiated in the processes of nature. Thus all becoming is organic becoming, passage from "possibility" to "realization," the development of an original capacity which persists as unity and wholeness unfolding itself unto its parts.

The mathematical science of nature was vigorously opposed to this anthropomorphism and refused to return to it. Still, if the whole, as goal-directed and goal-pursuing *force,* had dropped out [of science], the *category* of wholeness had not. To be sure, mechanism had renounced even this category. It was to proceed analytically; that is, it had declared that the motion of a whole can only be understood when we have broken it up into the motion of its least parts and completely reduced it to this. Lagrange's *Analytical Mechanics* is the outstanding attempt to carry through this program. Looked at philosophically, it necessarily contained the ideal of that "Laplacian mind," capable of surveying forward and backward the totality of world events, by knowing in a given moment the position of all individual mass-points and the laws for the motion of these points. However, in the course of their development, classical physics and point-mechanics were led to problems which they were not able to handle with this methodology. They

were forced to concede to a reconstruction of their conceptual apparatus which made more and more questionable
the assumption that every whole must admit of being understood as the "sum of its parts." Here the Faraday-Max-
well concept of the electromagnetic field was the decisive
turning point. A penetrating picture of how the old "substance theory" has been superseded by the modern "field
theory" has been given by Hermann Weyl in his book,
What Is Matter? He finds the essential and epistemologically important difference between the two in the fact that
the field itself no longer admits of being understood as a
merely additive whole, an aggregate of parts. The field is
not a thing-concept but a concept of relation; it is not com-
posed of pieces but is a system, a totality of lines of force.

> For field theory, a material particle, such as the elec-
> tron, is merely a small area of the electrical field in
> which the strength of the field assumes an enormously
> high value and where there is, consequently, an intense
> concentration of field force. This scheme of the world
> reduces to a complete continuum. Even atoms and elec-
> trons are not ultimate unchanging elements shoved
> willy nilly by bombarding forces of nature, but are
> themselves subject to continuous, extended, and deli-
> cately flowing changes.[2]

The return to the concept of the whole emerges still
more clearly and characteristically in the development of
biology. Occasionally the swing back to it goes so far that a
complete restitution of the concept in its original Aristo-

2. Hermann Weyl, *Was ist Materie?* (Berlin: J. Springer, 1924),
p. 35.

telian meaning appears to have been achieved. At first glance vitalism may be taken as nothing other than a remarkable Aristotelian renaissance, which gives the appearance of taking biological science, at least, back to its first beginnings. Driesch's concept of entelechy is tied directly to Aristotle's, both in name and in fact. Nevertheless, if one follows the overall movement of biological thought in the last decades, it becomes evident that here, too, in spite of the extreme nearness to the Aristotelian concept of form, there followed a differentiation and splitting within the content of the concept, similar to that which we were able to detect in the thinking of physicists. The category of wholeness no longer corresponds exactly to that of end but begins definitely to sever itself from it. In the first beginnings of the vitalist movement problems of form still run together indiscriminately with problems of causation. Here it is believed that it is only possible to handle these problems without prejudice in this way: one must invoke another kind of causality than that which we encounter in the phenomena of the inorganic world. Thus, where one sees restitution and regeneration, where one finds maintenance and reproduction of specific structure and character in the biological world, one discovers *forces* different from the mechanical, and necessarily superior to them. So Driesch avails himself of the phenomena of restitution and regeneration in his attempt to revive the concept of living force. For him, the soul again becomes an "elemental factor of nature." It does not belong to the spacial world, though it affects it. The entelechy cannot create any differences in intensity; but, where such differences in intensity already exist, it may well have the capacity to "suspend," i.e., to prevent, its effectiveness temporarily. Driesch believed he was able to reconcile this basic view with the law of the conservation of energy and to show that purely physical balance of forces in nature was not altered by the introduction of this new "psychic" force.[3] But his theory is and remains a purely metaphysical doctrine, which quickly forgets the experiential basis on which it rests. Modern biology has not followed Driesch. But neither has it reverted to the "machine theory of life." It has avoided both extremes while concerning itself more and more with the purely methodological significance of the problem. For it, the primary question is not whether organic forms can be *explained* by means of purely mechanical forces; instead the emphasis falls on the fact that organic forms cannot be fully *described* through purely causal concepts. In demonstrating this it invokes the category of "wholeness."

One gets some idea of the state of the problem in the extremely comprehensive survey of theoretical biology which Ludwig von Bertalanffy has given.[4] Bertalanffy insists that, in each of the natural sciences, progress in clarification of concepts is equally as necessary as progress in factual knowledge. He finds one of the most significant advances in the former in the fact that biology has learned to carry out the study of wholeness with exactness, and without slipping into the path of teleological considerations and without losing itself in the assumption of "final causes." The phenomena of organic nature do not demonstrate such causes; they show us no "entelechy" in Driesch's sense, no "transcendent powers" in Eduard von Hartmann's sense, and no "dom-

3. Cf. Hans Driesch, *Sie Seele als elementar Naturfaktor* (Leipzig: W. Engelmann, 1903); *The Science and Philosophy of Organism* (London: Adam and Charles Black, 1908), II, 219 f. and *passim*.

4. Ludwig von Bertalanffy, *Theoretische Biologie* (Berlin: Gebrüder Borntraeger, 1932), Vol. I.

inants" in Reinke's sense. All they show us is that the events
in the organism continually maintain a specific orientation.

The individual processes which play themselves out
within the organism can certainly be described physically and chemically; but this by no means characterizes them as living processes. Most, if not all, life-
processes show themselves to be so ordered as to be
directed toward the maintenance and restitution of the
whole. . . . Actually there can be no doubt whatever
concerning the fact that the phenomena in the organism are, by and large, "holistic" and "system-maintain-
ing" and that it is the task of biology to establish the
fact that, and the extent to which, this is the case. Following old modes of thought, some called this ordered
property of life "purposiveness" and sought for the
"end" of an organ or of a function. But a desiring or
intending of goals always appeared to be involved in
the concept of "end"—a mode of representation to
which the natural scientist is justly unsympathetic;
and hence the attempt was made to restrict purposiveness as a merely subjective and unscientific mode of
observation. Actually, in its absolute formulation, the
holistic mode of study has been as abused as was the
"study of purposiveness," first in Darwinism, which set
up numerous, totally untenable hypotheses concerning
"purposiveness" in its efforts to discover utility-values
and selection-values for every organ and characteristic,
and secondly in Vitalism, which looked upon "purposiveness" as proof of the governing role of its vital factors.

But according to Bertalanffy this misuse need not prevent
us from recognizing that concern for wholeness has its

rightful and necessary place in the development of biology and that it cannot be supplanted by any other methods. Also, it can in no way be meant to suppress or make superfluous a knowledge of causal connections. "There is no sense in trying to deny the maintenance of wholes in organic phenomena; the correct procedure is first to discover this maintenance and then to explain it."[5]

That modern *psychology* has also followed the same line of development, that the tendency which can be shown in physics and biology is particularly clear in psychology, is scarcely in need of proof. At the very least, psychology appears to have seen this *methodological problem* sooner than the other sciences. But it was not immediately able to tackle it, for its own past, its entire scientific history, stood in its way. As an empirical science, psychology was an infant, an offshoot of natural research. Its first task was necessarily to free itself from the domination of Scholastic concepts, just as the other sciences had done, and to take note of the fundamental facts of mental life. But there appeared to be no other path leading to these fundamental facts than that along which exact science had proved itself. Thus, at the hands of its first scientific founders, the methodology of psychology was patterned after that of physics. Accordingly, Hobbes consciously endeavored to transport Galileo's "resolutive and compositive" method from the domain of physics to that of psychology. In the eighteenth century, it is Condillac's ambition to become the "Newton of psychology," by availing himself of Newton's method—the anal-

5. In this statement of the ideals of biological knowledge Bertalanffy bases himself, above all, on J. S. Haldane, who has introduced the term "holism" for this position. Cf. Haldane's *New Physiology* (London: Ch. Griffin and Company, 1919) and Adolf Mayer, *Ideen und Ideale der biologischen Erkenntniss* (Leipzig, 1934).

ysis of all complex phenomena into a simple and basic phenomenon.[6] Not only all the various contents of consciousness, but also all the observable activities themselves, all the
operations and processes of consciousness, are to be completely deducible from it.[7]

With this psychology had become the psychology of elements, for which point-mechanics was, and remains, the il-
lustrious model. Just as astronomy discovered the fundamental laws of the universe by studying the laws which hold
for motion of simple mass-points, so psychology must deduce all mental life from "atoms of sensation" and from the
rules of their conjunction, from "perceptions" and "asso-
ciations." The reality of consciousness is to be explained
only in terms of its genesis, and this genesis, in the final
analysis, is nothing else, and nothing more complex, than
combination of homogeneous parts into ever more complex
structures. The manner and means through which modern
psychological research has overturned this view are well
known. To be sure, in doing so, it not only has not abandoned genetic problems but has even given them a new significance. But it no longer contends that these problems
constitute the only subject matter of psychology, or that its
content is coextensive with these problems. Over against
the concept of cause there emerges the *concept of structure*
as the dominant principle. Structure is not understood, it
is destroyed, when the attempt is made to analyze it into a
mere aggregate, a "summation." Here, too, the concept of
"wholeness" is accorded its rightful place, its fundamental

6. Cf. Georges Le Roy, *La Psychologie de Condillac* (Paris: Boivin
& Co., 1937).

7. For further details see my *Philosophy of the Enlightenment*,
trans. Fritz C. A. Koelln and James P. Pettegrove (Princeton: Princeton University Press, 1951), pp. 17 ff.

importance is acknowledged; the psychology of elements has become Gestalt psychology.

We have referred to these methodological transformations within physics, biology, and psychology only in order to ascertain the extent to which the comparison can throw added light on the development of the "scientific" study of the humanities [*der Kulturwissenschaften*]. This problem can now be grasped with more clarity and can be given a surer answer. Recognition of the concept of wholeness and of the concept of structure has in no way eliminated or obliterated the difference between the natural sciences and the humanities. But it has removed a separating partition which, until now, has stood between them. The "scientific" study of the humanities can abandon itself to consideration of *its own forms* and *its own structures* with greater freedom and less restraint than heretofore as a consequence of the fact that the other fields of knowledge have become more mindful of their own very real problems of form. The logic of research is able now to assign each of these problems to its rightful place. Form-analysis and causal analysis are now seen to be orientations which, instead of contending with each other, complement each other, and which necessarily require each other in all knowledge.

The phenomena of culture show themselves to be even more tenaciously bound to the sphere of becoming than are the phenomena of nature. They are unable to leave the stream of process. We cannot pursue linguistics, art analysis, or the study of religion without basing our work on what we are able to learn from the history of language, art history, and the history of religion. Nor can we venture out upon these high seas of becoming without relying on the compass of categories of "cause" and "effect." The phenomena remain one unsurveyable confusion until we bind them

together with fixed causal chains. This eagerness to penetrate into the causal relations of the genesis of culture is so
strong that it easily makes us lose sight of all other considerations. Nevertheless, analysis of the genesis of culture and
its causal explanation is not the whole of its study. It is only
a single *dimension* of the science of cultural events; other
dimensions, equally justified and equally autonomous,
stand in contrast to it. Our awareness of culture first acquires its true depth when we differentiate all these dimensions in order that, on the basis of this differentiation, their
true unity may be understood. There are three factors
which it is possible to isolate here and which must be carefully distinguished. In all study of human achievements,
analysis as achievement, analysis as process (which resides
essentially in the study of cause and effect), and *analysis as
form* stand out as distinct from each other.

It is the [pragmatic] analysis of works which constitutes
the true bedrock. For, before we can write a cultural history
and before we can construct any representation of the causal
connections of its individual phenomena, we must have an
overall view of the *achievements* of language, art, and religion. It is not enough that we have it before us as mere
raw material. It is necessary that we penetrate its *significance;* we must understand what it has to say to us. This
understanding possesses its own method of explanation—
an autonomous, most difficult, and complex "hermeneutic." When, as a result of this hermeneutic, the confusion
begins to recede, when ever-clearer, specific, and basic forms
[*Grundgestalten*] begin gradually to be distinguishable in
the monuments of culture, when certain classes begin to
group themselves together, when we are able to discover
fixed orderings and relationships within these classes—
when this occurs, a new and twofold task begins. Broadly

speaking it consists in determining the "what" of each *distinct form* of culture—the "nature" of language, religion, and art. First, what "is," and what is the meaning, of each of them? And what functions do they fulfill? Second, how are language, myth, art, and religion related to each other? What distinguishes them and what binds them to each other? Here we arrive at a "theory" of culture which, in the end, must seek its realization in a Philosophy of Symbolic Forms; and this realization is to be conceived in terms of an "infinitely distant point" which we can approach only asymptotically.

From the analysis of form we advance to that procedure which we can characterize as *act-analysis*. This is not a question as to the achievements, the works, of culture; nor is it a question as to the general forms in which they present themselves to us. Our question concerns the mental *processes* from which they have come into being and whose product they are. What we are looking for here is, for example, the character of that "consciousness of symbols" which makes itself known in the act of human speech; we are inquiring into the manner and orientation of the building of representations, feelings, fantasies, and beliefs in which art, myth, and religion *have their being*.

Each of these modes of observation has its claim and its necessity. In terms of logic, each makes use of distinct instruments and categories which belong specifically to it.

We must be clear about all this and constantly bear it in mind if we are to avoid the quarrels over boundaries, and distortions of boundaries, which have never ceased to crop up in the humanities and in the philosophy of culture. One of the most notorious examples of this is [to be seen in] the question as to the origins of language, myth, art, and religion. The difficulty arises from the fact that we apply the lever of causal inquiry at the wrong place. Instead of being applied to the phenomena *within* a specific form, it has been applied to the form as such, as if it were a self-enclosed whole. But here the category of cause and effect—so indispensable and fruitful in its proper sphere—leaves us in the lurch. Closer inspection shows those solutions, which it claims to give, to be tautologies and vicious circles. Linguistics and philosophy of language have continually sought to clear up the obscurity of the "origin" of language. But if one surveys the various theories which they have advanced, one gets the impression that they have not made the least bit of progress. If one is determined to have language arise from nature through some intermediate stage, there is nothing to do but tie it immediately to specific phenomena of nature. Thus, before it could be explained as a mental process, it would have to be explained as an organic process.

What this comes to is that we have traced the true origin of language to pure sensation of sound. The cry of pain and anguish, the coaxing or the warning call—these appear to be spread over large parts of the animal world. The problem [of grounding speech in nature] does give the *appearance* of being solved if the bridge can be built here, if it can be shown that interjections constitute the true source and the "principle" of speech.

But of necessity it soon became evident that this was a vain hope. For in all this the most important factor has been ignored. Just what *remains unexplained* is how the cry becomes a "word," how it comes to have the power of *objective reference*. Here a second theory made its appearance. It was based on imitation of sounds and it regarded this as the earliest source of spoken words. But it also falls short of the basic phenomenon of speech—the appearance of the *sentence*. Thus, it failed by attempting to explain the sentence as a mere aggregate of words; as soon as the sentence was viewed in its actual "articulation," it was obvious that there is no structure in nature that corresponds to this articulation. Nor can recourse to "primitive" stages of speech show us the transition; for each linguistic phenomenon, however primitive, already contains the whole of language within itself, inasmuch as each sentence encloses the *function* of "signification" and "meaning" within itself.

From this it becomes immediately evident that at this point a fixed limit surrounds the reach of causal explanation. The function of speech, just as that of art, religion, etc., is and remains an *"Urphänomen"* [an irreducible fact], in the Goethian sense. It "appears and is"; there is nothing more in it still to be explained. As Goethe once remarked to Eckermann,

> The height of human attainment is amazement; and if the object of a man's amazement is an *Urphänomen*, he will have attained tranquility; he can have no higher awareness and he ought not to seek anything beyond it; for here is the absolute limit. But to average human beings contemplation of an *Urphänomen* is not enough; they think there must be something beyond; they are like children who, upon peeping into a mirror, instantly turn it over to see that which lies on the other side.[8]

The objection may be raised: Is not this "turning over," in all likelihood, the true task of *philosophy*, which, unlike

___

8. February 18, 1829: J. P. Eckermann, *Gespräche mit Goethe*, 6th ed. (Leipzig: F. A. Brockhaus, 1885), II, 50 f.

art, cannot rest content with the simple intuition and with the appearance, but which must penetrate, instead, to the idea, to the ground of the phenomenal world? Was it not just this reorientation in vision which Plato insisted upon, and which he depicted so characteristically and suggestively in his Myth of the Cave in the *Republic?* If philosophy and science forbid asking why on such a weighty and decisive issue, will they not have surrendered to skepticism? Can they ever afford to part with the "principle of sufficient reason"?

Such abandonment is in fact unnecessary. Instead, what *is* necessary is that we continue to remain clearly mindful of the fact that skepticism also has its rightful claim. For skepticism is not simply denial or destruction of knowledge. Philosophy itself serves as proof of this. One needs only to think of its most significant and fruitful periods in order to realize what an important and indispensable role has been played by *knowing-not* and how, time and again, knowledge was only able to find and renew itself by means of it. The Socratic [awareness of] knowing-not, Nicholas of Cusa's *Docta Ignorantia,* and the Cartesian doubt are among the most important instruments of philosophic knowledge. It is better to be without knowledge on some point than to be blind to a problem because we have contented ourselves with an apparent solution. All genuine skepticism is relative skepticism. It denies that certain questions are genuinely soluble problems in order to be better able to point out those problems which are soluble and in order to get a surer grip on them.

So it is with our problem. What it demands of us is not that we give up asking why, but that we apply the question properly. What is to be learned here—at bottom it is what physics, biology, and psychology are all able to teach us—

is that we must not confuse the question of structure with the question of cause, that the one cannot be reduced to the other. Each has its limited claim; each is necessary and indispensable; and neither can fulfill the function of the other. Once we have ascertained the "essence" of language by means of the method of form-analysis, we must then attempt to find out, by way of causal knowledge (the way of the psychology of speech and the history of language) just how it is that this essence develops and transmutes itself. In doing so we are wholly concerned with a case of pure becoming; but this becoming remains within the determinate frame of being; for always it remains within that "structure" which is language. As such, it is, as Plato put it, "becoming within being," γένεσις εἰς οὐσίαν. Here the concept of form and the concept of causality are set apart from each other in order that each may be more securely reclaimed and in order that they may be all the more closely tied to each other. The union of both can only be fruitful for empirical research if each maintains its rightful place and its independence.

When this is clearly understood, having to concede that the question of the *origin of the symbol function* is not soluble by causal means will, by no means, appear to be a mere agnosticism, an intellectual sacrifice to be exacted at all cost. What it affirms is, not that we stand here at an absolute limit of our knowledge, but rather that knowledge of coming-to-be does not exhaust the whole of knowledge, that next to it there exists *another form of knowledge, concerned* not with coming-to-be [nor with passing-away] but *simply with duration*. The dead end only makes its appearance when we assume that the concepts of cause and effect are the only guides to knowledge and that where they fail us there can only be obscurity and ignorance. As we have seen, Hobbes has even made this "axiom" the defining concept of *philosophy*.[9] But what is set up here as the principle of knowledge is, in fact, only a begging of the question. Thus, it takes as proved the very point which constitutes the real problem and which is what is most in need of proof. Its starting point is that, in addition to that dimension which is defined and dominated by the concept of causality, there is no other plane in which there is anything whatever to be "known." What has continually impeded and held up acceptance of the multi-dimensionality of knowledge is that with its acceptance the principle of evolution appears to come to nothing. In fact there is no "evolution" which logically leads from the one dimension to the other [from the dimension of causal nexus to that of meaning, of purely formal structure]. At any particular point, a generic distinction must be made which can only be posited, without admitting of further explanation. At present, to be sure, this problem, too, has lost much of its sting. For even in *biology* our accepted interpretation of the theory of evolution no longer has each new form deriving from the old by mere accumulation of chance variations. Today, the Darwinian theory, which once sought to carry through this interpretation because of its predilection for the principle of continuity, is probably no longer defended by any biologist in the form which dogmatic Darwinism gave to it.

As a result, the thesis, *"natura non facit saltus,"* underwent a most essential qualification. Its problematic nature has been disclosed in quantum theory in the field of physics and in mutation theory in the field of biology. For in the organic sphere "evolution" remains nothing but an empty

9. Supra, p. 163.

word if we are to assume that what is involved is a mere "unfolding" of a given and finished being, as in the old theories of preformation and involution, where, in the end, every new form is enclosed within the old. Here, too, at each point we must acknowledge something novel, something not arrived at without a "gap." Indeed, this is Hugo de Vries' own characterization of his mutation theory:

> I define mutation theory as the thesis that the characteristics of organisms are built from wholes sharply distinct from each other. . . . In the field of evolutionary theory this principle leads to the conviction that species do not flow [into one another] but have originated from one another in a stepwise fashion. Each new whole coming from the old constitutes a break which sharply and completely distinguishes the new form as a species independent from the species from which it came. The new species comes into being immediately; it arises from the earlier one without detectable preparation and without transition.[10]

In *this* respect, the transition from nature to "culture" does not present us with any new riddles. It merely verifies what the study of nature has taught us—that every genuine development is at bottom, a μετάβασις εἰς ἄλλογένος, which, to be sure, we *can exhibit,* but which [as such] cannot be given any further causal explanation. Here experience and thought, the empirical method and philosophy, find themselves in the same circumstance. For each is un-

10. Hugo de Vries, *The Mutation Theory,* trans. J. B. Farmer and A. D. Darbishire (Chicago: The Open Court Publishing Company, 1909), I, 3.

able to determine that "in-itself" of human nature except by *exhibiting* it within the phenomena. They cannot attain knowledge of the "essence" of man, except by viewing man in culture, in the mirror of culture; nor can they turn this mirror over to see what lies behind it.

CHAPTER 5

The "Tragedy of Culture"

HEGEL HAS SAID that world history is not the dwelling place of good fortune, that peaceful and happy periods are empty pages in the book of history. For him, this in no way contradicted his basic conviction that "everything in history takes place in accordance with reason"; instead, he regarded it as confirmation and sanction for that basic conviction. But what is the meaning of the triumph of the idea if it has to be bought at the sacrifice of all human happiness? Doesn't such a theodicy sound almost like sarcasm, and wasn't Schopenhauer right when he declared Hegelian "optimism" to be not only an absurd but even a reckless way of thinking? Time and again such questions have presented themselves to the human mind and in the very midst of the richest and most spectacular periods of civilization. Here, instead of finding enrichment, people have looked upon culture as an ever growing estrangement from the true goals of existence.

At the midpoint of the Enlightenment, Rousseau brought forth the flaming indictment of his "discourse against the arts and sciences": the arts and sciences have morally weakened and unnerved the human race; physically, they have not satisfied human needs; instead, they have aroused thousands of insatiable desires; all the values of culture and civilization are phantoms, which we must renounce if we are not to be forever led astray, forever drinking from the cask of futility. With this accusation, Rousseau shook eighteenth century rationalism to its very foundations. Here lay that profound influence which he exercised upon Kant. For Kant saw himself freed by Rousseau from mere intellectualism and given a new orientation. He no longer believed that advance and refinement of intellectual pursuits could solve the riddle of existence and heal all the ills of human society. Mere cultivation of the mind could not justify the ultimate worth of mankind; this must be governed and controlled by other powers. But if a balance between the intellectual and the moral has been attained, and if, moreover, practical reason is given primacy over theoretical reason, the hope that the demand for human happiness can be fulfilled is as vain as ever. Kant is thoroughly convinced of the "abortiveness of all philosophical attempts at theodicy." For him there remains no other solution than that radical rejection of eudaemonism which he attempted in the groundwork of his ethics. If happiness were the true goal of human striving, culture would have its justification, once and for all. For Kant, however, justification of culture can only lie in some other measure of value; true worth does not lie in that which man receives from nature and Providence; it resides only in his own acts and in what he creates through these acts.

With this Kant has assumed Rousseau's basic premise without drawing the same conclusion. Rousseau's call, "Back to nature!" was supposed to be able to restore and assure happiness to mankind; but at the same time it estranged man from his true nature. For his true nature resides not in the sensuous but in the intelligible. Not happiness but the condition of being worthy of happiness ["*Glückswürdigkeit*"] is what culture [and civilization] promises to man; it cannot give him more. Its goal is not the realization of happiness in this life, but the realization of freedom—that genuine autonomy which consists, not in the technical dominance of man over nature, but man's moral mastery of himself.

In this Kant believed that he had transformed the theodicy problem from a metaphysical to an ethical problem and that by virtue of this transformation he had given the problem a critical solution. Still, not all the doubts which can be levelled against the value of culture are to be stilled by such a transformation.

For another and much deeper conflict emerges when one studies the new goal which culture assumes at this juncture. Can this goal actually be attained? Is it certain that man can find his "intelligible" essence in culture and cultural fulfillment, that here he will attain, not the satisfaction of all his wishes, to be sure, but the development of all his spiritual powers and talents? This would only be the case if man were able to go beyond the limits of his individuality, if he were able to identify his ego with the whole of mankind. But in this very attempt he feels his limitations all the more clearly and painfully. For here, too, there exists a factor which threatens and suppresses the pure self-sufficiency of the ego, instead of enlarging and heightening it.

Only when we are actually involved in this side of the problem does it attain its full force. In an essay entitled "The Concept and Tragedy of Culture" Georg Simmel has stated the problem with complete decisiveness. But he doubts that it has any solution. According to him, philosophy is only able to point out the conflict; it cannot claim any ultimate way out of the difficulty. For the deeper it penetrates the more does philosophic reflection reveal a *dialectical structure within our consciousness of culture.* The advance of culture continually presents man with new gifts; but the individual sees himself more and more cut off from the enjoyment of them. And what is the good of all this wealth which no single self can ever transmute into its own living possession? Instead of being liberated, is not the individual ego merely burdened by it? In such considerations we first encounter cultural pessimism in its sharpest and most radical formulation. For it now touches upon a point of extreme sensitivity. It points to a defect from which no intellectual development can free us, for the defect is inherent to the very nature of intellectual development. The goods which it creates continually grow in number; but it is in this very growth that they lose their value for us. They become mere objects—merely ready and given things which no longer admit of being involved within the ego and comprehended by it. The ego finds itself smothered in the midst of their multiplicity and their continually accelerating domination. The ego no longer draws from culture the consciousness of its own power; it draws only the certainty of its impotence.

Simmel sees the real cause of this "Tragedy of Culture" in the fact that the seeming intensification which culture promises us is forever accompanied by a species of abandonment of self. Between soul and world there persists a continuous relationship of tension, which in the end threatens to become a relationship of complete antithesis. Finally, man cannot make gains even into the spiritual world without suffering injury to his soul. Spiritual life consists in continuous advance; but the life of the soul consists in an ever deeper return into itself. The goals and the

ways of "objective spirit" can never, therefore, be the same
as those of the subjective life. Whatever the individual soul
is no longer able to pervade becomes nothing but a hard
shell. This shell continues to thicken and encompass the
soul, with less and less likelihood of weakening.

In contrast to life, vibrating, restless, endlessly self-
evolving, soul—in some sense the creative force—
stands [also] as life's fixed, ideal, and immovable product, whose uncanny counter-effect is to fix, indeed, to
freeze all vitality; it is as if the creative motion of the
soul were always to die in its products. . . . Although
the logic of impersonal constructions and relationships
is full of dynamics, between it and the drives and
norms of personality there insue points of extreme
friction, which attain a singular intensity in the form
of culture as such. When the human being says "I" to
himself, he has become an object both to and above
himself; ever after, and through this form our soul
belongs to its contents, as being their center; and ever
after, within it, and from this form, all that is ideal
must take its growth, with the result that with its ties
to this center all that is ideal is also a unity, self-enclosed and therefore a self-sufficient whole. But the
contents with which the ego is supposed to perfect this
organization into a truly unified world do not belong
merely to the ego; they are *given* to it by one mode or
another of externality—spacial, temporal, or ideal;
they are, then, at the same time, the contents of another world—be it social, metaphysical, conceptual,
ethical—and within these other worlds they possess
forms and relations which refuse to be united with
those of the ego. . . . This is the real tragedy of culture.

For we define a tragic fate—in contradistinction to one which is pitiable or comes as destruction from external causes—as one in which the destroying forces are not only directed against a being but originate in the deepest recesses of this very being; it is a fate in which a destiny is completed in a self-destruction which is latent and, so to speak, the logical development of the very structure by means of which that being has attained its positive existence.[1]

In this presentation the suffering with which all human culture is afflicted appears to be even deeper and more hopeless than Rousseau had depicted it. For even that return which Rousseau sought and demanded is of no avail here. Simmel is far from wishing to arrest the advance of civilization at some particular stage. He knows that the wheel of history cannot be turned back. But, at the same time, he is sure that the tension between the two equally necessary and equally valid poles will become ever more tense and that finally mankind will have to resign itself to an incurable dualism. The deep estrangement and animosity which obtain between the living, creative process of the soul, on the one hand, and its contents and creations, on the other, admit of no balance and no reconciliation. In order to make itself more intelligible and more tangible, this process must become ever richer and more intensive and extend itself over an ever wider sphere.

Here Simmel seems to speak the language of the skeptic; but, in fact, he is speaking the language of the mystic. For it is the secret yearning of every mystic to become purely

---

1. Georg Simmel, *Philosophische Kultur* (Leipzig: A. Kröner, 1911), pp. 251 ff.

and solely absorbed in the essence of the I, in order to find
in it the essence of God. What lies between self and God
they can only regard as a separation. This is no less true of
the spiritual world than it is of the physical world. For
spirit itself exists only by virtue of the fact that it is always
and forever discarding itself. It is ceaselessly fashioning new
names and new creations; but it fails to realize that in its
creations it is not approaching the divine, but wandering
further and further from it. The mystic must turn against
the entire creative world of culture. He must free himself
from "name and image." He demands that we relinquish
and smash all symbols. He does not act in the hope that we
will in this way come *to know* God. The mystic knows and
is profoundly inspired by the fact that all *knowing* is possible only in the sphere of symbols. It is a different and higher
goal which he has set for himself. His desire is that the I,
instead of vainly attempting to conceive and grasp the divine, become dissolved into the divine, come to be at one
with it. Here all plurality is deception—regardless of
whether it is a plurality of things or of signs and images.

Nevertheless, even as the mystic says this, as he *appears*
to give up all claim to a substantial existence of his own individuality, in so doing he has, in one sense, held on to and
sanctioned such *substantiality*. For he has assumed selfhood
to be something determinate in itself, something self-sufficient, and not to be lost to the world. But this raises the
first question which we must ask of the mystic. In an earlier
remark we sought to show that the "I" does not exist as an
original and given reality, which relates itself to other realities of the same kind, thus entering into communion with
them. We found ourselves obliged to give this relationship
a different interpretation. We found that separation between "I" and "you," and likewise that between "I" and

"world" constitutes the goal and not the starting point of the spiritual life.

If we stick to this interpretation, our problem takes on a new significance. For that consolidation which life undergoes in the various forms of culture—in language, religion, and art—is not the absolute *antithesis* to that which the I requires by its very nature; instead it is the very *condition* by virtue of which it discovers and comes to know its own being. Here we encounter a relation of the highest complexity, which cannot be appropriately represented by spacial imagery, however subtle. It will not do to ask [what the mystic assumes] how the ego can go beyond its own sphere and enter one foreign to it. All such metaphorical expressions must be avoided.

To be sure, in the history of the problem of knowledge men have continually made use of such imperfect description in their efforts to characterize the relation of subject to object. It has been assumed that some part of the object must enter the I, in order for that object to be known. The image theory of the ancient atomists was rooted in this notion; Aristotle's theory of species, and that of the Scholastics, held to it, by merely translating the material images into mental images. But if we admit that such a miracle can take place—that the "object" can migrate into consciousness—the real problem remains forever unsolved; for what we still do not know is how this trace of the object, as it imprints itself upon the I, becomes *known* for what it is. The mere fact of its being there, and in just this way, by no means suffices as an explanation of its representative *significance*. This difficulty is still more acute when the importation is not from object to subject, but is to be realized between different subjects. Here again, it would be the luckiest of coincidence that one and the same content, a duplicate, should exist in "me" and in "another." But by virtue of what can the "I" know this same content as *from* the "you," or the "you" know it as *from* the "I"? How can one know this content to be *meant* as "coming" *from another?* This remains as unintelligible as ever.

What is still more telling is that mere passive "impression" is not capable of explaining the phenomenon of "expression." This constitutes one of the chief weaknesses of every sensationalist theory which argues that an ideal concept can be reduced to a copy of something objectively present. Thus one person is not recognized or understood by another by merely passing into that other person but by engaging him in an active give-and-take. We showed earlier that this is the meaning of all spiritual communication— that communication *as such* requires a sharing [*Gemeinschaft*], not of mere identity of products, but of specific processes.

This observation puts the problem raised by Simmel into fresh perspective. As such, it by no means ceases to exist; but now its solution must be sought in a different direction. The doubts and objections that can be raised against civilization continue in full force. We must be reasonable and admit that civilization is no harmonious self-enclosed whole, but is filled with the most violent inner tensions. Civilization is "dialectical," as well as dramatic. It is no simple event, no peaceful unwinding. Instead, it is an act, which it is forever necessary to begin anew; and its goal is never certain. Hence civilization can never abandon itself absolutely to a naive optimism or to a dogmatic belief in the "perfectibility" of man. For all that it has created it continually threatens to tear apart again with its own hands. Accordingly, when considered solely in the light of its products, it always contains something unsatisfactory, something which is profoundly questionable.

Truly productive minds put all their passion into their work; but this very passion continually becomes the source of new afflictions. It is this drama which Simmel has sought to depict. But he has recognized only two roles in it. On one side stands life and on the other side stands the sphere of ideal, self-justifying objective values. The two factors are never able to come into complete interaction or permeate each other. The further the cultural process develops, the more the created shows itself to be the enemy of the creator. Not only can the individual not fulfill himself in his work; in the end, his work threatens to destroy him. What life truly and inwardly strives for is nothing other than its own movement and the streaming fullness of it. It cannot bring forth this inner fullness, it cannot enable it to become perceptible in specific creations, except that these very creations become limits for it—firm embankments against which this motion streams and on which it breaks itself.

The mind brings forth countless creations, which exist apart in genuine self-sufficiency, as independent of the soul which created them as they are from each other and which the soul either accepts or rejects. Thus does the individual find himself opposed, just as art opposes law, as religion opposes science, as technology opposes custom. . . . It is as a result of this fixity of form, of the frozen state, of enduring existence, that spirit, in thus becoming object, opposes itself to the streaming vitality, the inner self-vindication, and the changing tensions of the individual soul. Thus is one mind inwardly united to another, but countless trag-

edies are played out as a result of and within this deep
opposition of forms—opposition between the subjective life, restless and temporally finite, and its content,
which, once created, is motionless, and its value time-
less.[2]

It would be futile to attempt to deny these tragedies or
to make light of them through some superficial means of
consolation. Nevertheless, they do take on a different appearance if we hold to the analysis outlined above and
pursue it to the end. For this path does not lead to the
work [in isolation], that enduring presence into which the
creative process has frozen itself, but to the "you," the
other person who receives this work, incorporating it into
his own life and thence transforming it back into the medium from which it originates. Here, at last, we see what
kind of resolution is possible for the "tragedy of culture."
So long as the "antagonist" does not become evident to the
ego, the circle cannot be closed. For however significant,
however substantial, however at rest in itself and in its own
point of focus a work of culture may be, it is and remains
only a *point of passage*. It is no "absolute" touching the I,
but the bridge which leads from one I-pole to another. In
this there lies a real and most significant function. The *living process* of culture has its being in the very fact that it is
inexhaustible in its creation of such mediation and transaction.

If we regard this process exclusively or predominantly
from the standpoint of the *individual*, it always contains a
peculiarly twofold character. The artist, the scientist, the
founder of a religion, are able to perform truly great

2. Simmel, *Philosophische Kultur*, pp. 265 ff.

achievements only if they abandon themselves completely to their work, if they neglect their own being for it. But, as soon as it finally stands before its creator, the finished product is never simply a thing of satisfaction; it is, at the same time, a disappointment. It falls short of the original intuition from which it came into being. Its circumscribed actualization stands in contradiction to the fullness of possibilities which this intuition ideally concealed within itself. Not only the artist but the thinker, too, continually feels this insufficiency. And the very greatest thinkers nearly always appear to arrive at a point at which they finally despair of giving expression to their ultimate and deepest thoughts. In his *Seventh Letter* Plato declares that the highest reaches of thought are no longer accessible to words; they elude written statement and doctrinal teaching. Such judgments are understandable and necessary, coming as they do from the psychological processes of genius.

But for us [as recipients] such skepticism lessens, the greater, the more comprehensive, and the richer the work of art or philosophy to which we have abandoned ourselves. For we who receive it do not measure with the same criterion with which the author measures his work. Where he sees too little, we are overwhelmed by too much; where he perceives an inner inadequacy, we stand before an impression of inexhaustible fullness, which we will never be able to completely master. Both judgments are equally justified and equally necessary; for it is only in this genuine relation of mutual dependence that the work first achieves its immediate task. It becomes the mediator between I and you, not by transporting a finished content from one person to another, but by kindling in one what exists in another. And with this we also realize why the truly *great works* of culture *never* confront us as things absolutely fixed and

unchanging, shackling and stifling the free motion of the
spirit in their fixity. Their content has being for us only
by virtue of the fact that they must be continually possessed
anew and hence continually recreated.

The nature of this process is, perhaps, most clearly evident where author and audience are not individuals but
whole epochs. Every "renaissance" of a past culture fur-
nishes us an example of this. Any renaissance which deserves the name is never a mere receiving. It is never a
simple carrying forward or developing of goals belonging
to a former culture. Often it believes itself to be just this;
often it knows no higher goal than to be able to imitate as
closely as possible the model it follows. All periods of classicism, in this sense, have regarded the great art works of
the ancients as paradigms which can be imitated but never
equalled. But the genuine and great renaissances in world
history have always been triumphs of spontaneity, instead
of mere receptivity. The way in which these two factors
interlock and mutually condition each other constitutes
one of the most intriguing problems in the history of
thought. One can talk here of an historical dialectic; but
it is not a dialectic which conceals a contradiction within
itself; instead, it is given within and derives from the very
processes of cultural development. Whenever an individual, or indeed an entire age, is prepared to abandon itself
completely to another, always, it has *found* itself in a new
and deeper sense.

So long as a particular culture borrows only specific
materials from another, without the will or the capacity to
possess it in its genuine center, to enter into it in its authentic *form,* this fruitful reciprocal effect will not occur. At
best it remains a superficial borrowing of individual com-
ponents. But these do not become genuinely formative

powers or motives. Indeed, the existence of this limited type
of influence of antiquity can be established for the entire
Middle Ages. As early as the ninth century there exists a
"Carolingian Renaissance" in pictorial art and in literature. Likewise, the School of Chartres may be characterized
as a "medieval renaissance." But all this is to be distinguished, not only in degree but also in manner, from that
"reawakening of classical antiquity" which set in during
the first centuries of the Italian Renaissance. Petrarch is
frequently referred to as "the first modern man." But, paradoxical as it may sound, he earned this title only by virtue
of the fact that he found his way to a new and deeper understanding of antiquity. Through the medium of ancient language, art, and literature he glimpsed, once again, the life-
forms of antiquity; and in this contemplation his own original feel for life took shape. This genuine penetration into
what is one's own and what is foreign holds good for the
entire Italian Renaissance. Burckhardt has said of the Italian Renaissance that it never "concerned itself with antiquity except to use it as a means of expressing its own creative ideas."[3]

This process is inexhaustible; it is forever being resumed.
According to Petrarch we have always been "rediscovering"
the ancients; and each time it is new and different features
which have come to light. Antiquity for Erasmus is no
longer the same as for Petrarch. And, by turns, antiquity for
Rabelais and Montaigne, for Corneille and Racine, for
Winckelmann, Goethe, and Wilhelm von Humboldt constitutes a worthy succession to the meaning it had for Petrarch and later for Erasmus. Any really intrinsic identity

3. Jacob Burckhardt, *Geschichte der Renaissance in Italien,* 5th ed.
(Eslingen: Paul Neff Verlag, 1912), p. 39.

between them is out of the question. What is identical is this —that the renaissance movements in Italy, the Netherlands, France, and Germany, each discovered in antiquity an incomparable source of power when utilized as an aid in bringing its own ideas and ideals to maturity. The really great cultural epochs of the past are not taken as extraneous building blocks which stand out as features of a bygone time in a building of the present. Instead of being inert masses, they are the aggregation of powerful potential energies, which are only waiting for the moment when they are to reappear, making themselves felt with novel effect. Here again the thing created does not stand in opposition to or outside the creative process; on the contrary, new life continually floods into these "old forms," preserving them and "preventing their rigidification."

It is obvious, of course, that this ceaseless give and take between different cultures cannot occur without inner friction. This sharing can never become a true coalescence, for the counterforces can only be effective by continuing to pit themselves against each other. The most explosive tensions exist just where a perfect harmony appears to be reached or within reach. If we study the aftereffect of classical civilization, we find that it presents almost the perfect limiting case. All that is merely negative appears to be extinguished; the great productive forces appear to be pure and unhindered, able to exercise their steady and peaceful influence. But here, too, in this ideal instance there is no lack of conflicts—indeed, of irreconcilable opposites. The history of law gives clear testimony to the remarkable strength of Roman law and to how, over the centuries, it has repeatedly demonstrated this strength anew. But Roman law was not able to be creative without, at the same time, destroying a wealth of promising possibilities. The conflict between the "natural" sense of justice and customary national laws, on the one hand, and scholarly law, on the other hand, broke out again and again. If oppositions of this kind are regarded as tragic conflicts, then the expression, the "tragedy of culture," will doubtless retain its full claim.

But we are obliged to study not only the fact of conflict but also its cure, its genuine "catharsis," and this never ceases to make its appearance. Time and again, with increased damming of forces on one side there comes a release of novel and still more powerful forces. This tightening and letting go is evident in the struggle between diverse cultures and it exists to no less a degree in that struggle in which the individual is pitted against the whole, in which the titanic creative power of the individual is in conflict with forces which have as their goal the preservation and, in a sense, the immortalization of the *status quo*.

Creativity is forever in conflict with tradition. But here, too, it is wrong to paint the conflict in black and white—as if one side had a complete monopoly on values and the other side a total absence of values. Tendencies toward preservation are no less significant and just as indispensable as those which seek renewal; for renewal can only come to flower through being preserved, and preservation is possible only through self-renewal.

This interdependence is sharpest where the struggle between the two tendencies plays itself out in subterranean depths—depths at which conscious plans and efforts of individuals have no control; for at this depth, the individual is not conscious of the controlling forces. We have just such a phenomenon in the development and transformation of *language*. The bond of tradition is at its strongest here and it appears to allow only trifling scope to the creativity of the individual. The philosophy of language has been marked by an endless debate as to whether language is a product of "nature" or of established convention, whether it be φύσει or θέσει. But it matters very little which argument one sides with, whether one regards language as something objective or as something subjective, as something real or as mere convention; for, if it be the latter, one must supply it with some measure of force by which it can hold its own against what is merely arbitrary. The "nominalist" Hobbes insisted that truth resides not in things but in signs: *"veritas non in re, sed in dicto consistit."* But to this he adds that, once they are established, the signs are not to be changed, that the convention must be acceded to if human speech and understanding are to be possible at all.

Obviously, history of language gives the lie to this belief in inalterable meanings for linguistic concepts established once and for all. What it does show is that every living linguistic usage undergoes a continual change in meaning. The reason for this is that "language" never exists as a physical "thing," remaining one and the same and forever exhibiting the same constant "properties." Speech exists only in the act of speaking, and this is never executed under exactly the same conditions and in exactly the same manner. In his *Principles of the History of Language* Herman Paul has shown the importance of circumstance—that language exists only by virtue of the fact that it is passed on from one generation to the next. This transmission can never take place if the function and spontaneity of these factors is eliminated. The receiver does not take the gift as one accepts a stamped coin. For he cannot receive it except by *using* it, and to make use of it [as something passed down] is to give it a new stamp. So, too, teacher and pupil, parent and child, never speak precisely "the same" language. Paul regards this process of formation and transformation as one of the most significant factors in the history of any language.[4]

To be sure, this creating of language, which manifests itself only in deviation from a given model, is still far removed from true creativity. It is a change taking place in the substratum of language; still it is not an act stemming from the conscious or active use of new forces. But this last decisive step is also necessary if language is not to die. This renewal from within first achieves its full strength and intensity as language not only serves merely for the communication and transmission of an established cultural possession but becomes the expression of novel and distinct feelings for life. As such feeling permeates the language, it arouses all the unrecognized energies slumbering within it. What was merely change within the sphere of everyday speech now becomes a construction of novel form, which can go so far that, in the end, virtually the entire body of the language—the vocabulary, grammar, and stylistic features of the language—are seen to be transformed.

The great epochs of poetry have influenced the formation of language in just this way. Dante's *Divine Comedy* has not only given the epic new meaning and content; it also constitutes the birth of the *lingua volgare* of modern Italian. Time and again in the lives of the great artists there appear to have been moments in which this urge for rejuvenation of the language was sensed so keenly that the given language, the material which they were obliged to work with, seemed to weigh them down like chains. At such moments their skepticism regarding language breaks forth in full force. Even Goethe is not free of this skepticism; his statement of it is as telling as that of Plato. In a well-known

4. Herman Paul, *Principles of the History of Language,* trans. H. A. Strong (London: Longmans, Green and Co., 1891), pp. 15 f.

Venetian epigram he declares that, in spite of his best efforts, there is one skill he has never been able to master—
the ability to write German.

Und so verderb' ich unglücklicher Dichter
In dem schlechtesten Stoff leider nun Leben und Kunst.

[And so, unlucky poet that I am, it is my lot
to prostitute life and art to the worst of stuff.]

But we know what Goethe's art has made of this "worst
of stuff." The German language at Goethe's death is no
longer what it was at his birth. It has not only been enriched
in content and widened beyond its previous limitations; it
has matured into a new form; it now contains possibilities
of expression which a century earlier were totally unrecognized.

The same contrast appears repeatedly in other spheres.
The creative process must always satisfy two different conditions: on the one side, it must tie itself to something
existing and enduring, and, on the other, it must be receptive to new use and application—this alters what [in other
respects] remains the same. Only in this way does one
succeed in doing justice to both the objective and the
subjective demands [implicit in the creative act]. Likewise,
and in much the same way, the plastic artist finds his path
opened and prepared, even if he distrusts its "language."
For, every language exhibits a determinate vocabulary,
which it did not create instantaneously, and the same holds
for all modes of creative activity in the plastic arts. There
is a reservoir of formal elements for the painter, the sculptor, the architect, and there is a very real "syntax" for each
of these fields, much as there is a syntax in any language.
All this cannot be spontaneously invented. It is here that
tradition forever maintains its claim; for only through it

can that continuity of creative activity be realized and captured which is the basis of intelligibility in the plastic arts. To quote Gottfried Semper:

> Just as linguistic elements continually maintain their values and re-emerge through all subsequent transformations and elaborations of concepts in which they are involved; just as it is impossible for a new concept to instantaneously invent a new word without failing in its primary intention—that it be intelligible; so one cannot abandon or ignore . . . the primitive types and elements of art symbolism. . . . The same advantage which comparative linguistics and etymology afford the contemporary rhetorician are even greater in the case of the plastic artist who is familiar with the original meaning of the earliest symbols of "his language" and can account for the ways in which they transform themselves through history in form and meaning, as the art itself undergoes change.[5]

The tie to tradition is most readily evident in what we call technique in the various arts. It is subject to rules as fixed as in any other use of tools; for it is dependent upon the nature of the materials in which the artist works. Art and craft, imaginative activity and skill, have disengaged themselves only slowly; and it is precisely when artistic achievement is highest that we are likely to find a particularly intimate union between these two factors. No artist can really speak his language if he has not previously learned it through a relentless experience of give and take

5. Gottfried Semper, *Der Stil in den technischen und tecktonischen Künsten,* 2d ed. (Munich: F. Bruckmann, 1878), I, 6.

with its materials. And this is by no means restricted merely to the material-technical side of the problem. It also has its exact parallel in the sphere of form as such. For, once created, even the artistic forms become part of the fixed tradition handed down from one generation to another. Often this transmission and inheritance can stretch over centuries. Each age takes over fixed forms from its predecessor and hands them on to its successor. The language of forms assumes such fixity that specific themes, with their determinate modes of expression, seem so firmly grown together that we encounter them again and again in the same or only slightly modified forms.

This "law of inertia" governing the transfer of forms constitutes one of the most important factors in the development of art: it is one of the most engaging problems of art history. In recent times it is especially A. Warburg who has laid the greatest stress on this process and who has sought to throw light on it from all angles, psychological as well as historical. Warburg set out from a study of the art history of the Italian Renaissance. But for him it was only a unique paradigm within which he sought to clarify the *distinctive trait* and *basic orientation* of the creative processes involved in plastic art. He found both most clearly expressed in the survival of ancient forms. He showed how for certain typical, ever-recurring situations the ancients created specific pregnant forms of expression. It is not simply that certain inner excitations, certain tensions and resolutions are firmly adhered to; it is as if later artists are under their spell. Wherever the same feeling is suggested the old image which his art creates comes to life again. It arises, according to Warburg's expression, from determinate "feeling formulas" [*"Pathosformeln"*] indelibly stamped in the human memory. Warburg has pursued the duration and change, the statics and dynamics of these "feeling formulas" throughout the history of the visual arts.[6]

In his work Warburg has not only enriched the content of art history but has also given it a new methodological character. For here he has touched upon a basic systematic problem—one common to all critical inquiry within the humanities. Just as the painter and sculptor employ specific and fixed postures, arrangements, and gestures of the human body to give visible form to psychic presence and to the movement of the soul, so likewise in each of the other areas of culture there is this ever-present task of capturing motion and rest, change and duration, within unified wholes—of using the one factor as the presentational medium of the other. If they are "universal and communicable," if they are to form bridges between other selves, linguistic forms and art forms must of necessity possess inner fixity and consistency. But, at the same time, they must, of necessity, be capable of modification; for every *use* of form, before it can make its way from one person to another, already undergoes a certain modification, without which its use would be impossible.

The various species of art can be differentiated on the basis of the way in which these two universally necessary polar opposites are related within them. Here, of course, we are obliged to answer only a basic and preliminary question. Is there any sense whatever in which we are justified in speaking of such "species"? Are they anything more than merely verbal distinctions? Ancient poetics and rhetoric begin by drawing strict distinctions between the various

6. Cf. especially A. Warburg, "Die Eneuerung der heidnischen Antike: Kulturwissenschaftliche Beiträge zur Geschichte der europäische Renaissance," *Aby Warburg, Gesammelte Schriften* ed. by Gertrud Bing (Leipzig: G. B. Teubner, 1932).

forms of literary expression and by ascribing a determinate
and unalterable "nature" to each of them. It thought of the
individual poetic forms as *specifically* distinct, one from the
other, that the ode and the elegy, the idyl and the fable had
each its own objects and its own laws. Classical aesthetics
employs this view as its basic principle. Boileau holds (as
an unquestioned assumption) that comedy and tragedy
have each their own "essence" and that this "essence" of
necessity determines for each its choice of motive, its characters, and its linguistic devices. This fundamental notion
is dominant even with Lessing, though he gives it an in-
trinsically freer formulation. To the genius he grants the
prerogative of going beyond the limits of the various genres; nonetheless, he did not believe that these limits could
be denied [*aufgehoben*] in principle.

Modern aesthetics has attempted to treat all these fixed
distinctions as mere ballast which we must simply throw
overboard. Benedetto Croce has gone farthest in this direction. He has declared all classification of the arts and all
distinctions between species of art to be mere nomencla-
ture, which can serve a practical purpose but which lack
any theoretical significance. According to Croce, such clas-
sifications have only the value of the rubrics under which
we stack books in libraries. He insists that art does not
admit of being partitioned off into sections, either as things
are or on the basis of their mode of presentation. For him
the aesthetic synthesis is and remains an indivisible unity.

> Every work of art expresses a state of emotion; this
> state of emotion is always unique and original; so, too,
> the intuition signifies infinitely many intuitions, which
> it is impossible to reduce to a latticework of *species*.
> . . . It is evident from this that any theory which at-

tempts a *breakdown of the arts* has no basis whatsoever. The species or class is, in this case, a class of one—it is simply art or intuition; to be sure, the individual works of art are countless—though each is original, none can take the place of any other . . . each is beyond the reach of the understanding. In philosophic contemplation there is no middle factor between universal and particular, no spectrum of species or types, of *"generalia."* Neither the artist who creates the art, nor the viewer who contemplates it, has need of anything other than the universal and the particular, or, better still, the individual which has become universal—that universal artistic activity which has completely concentrated and gathered itself into the presentation of a single state of emotion.[7]

If this were true without qualification, it would lead one to the odd conclusion that by calling Beethoven a great musician, Rembrandt a great painter, Homer a great epic poet, and Shakespeare a great dramatist, we are merely referring to unimportant empirical circumstances, which have no *aesthetic* significance and have no bearing on their characterization as *artists.* Here there is only "the" art, on the one hand, and the particular, on the other. In this event, the medium in which a given artist seeks to express himself is purely accidental. It might just as well take place in colors or in tones, in words or in marble, without the intuition of the artist being affected; it would remain the same, except that it would have chosen a different kind of mediation in each instance.

7. Benedetto Croce, *Grundiss der Aesthetik,* German ed. (Leipzig: F. Meiner, 1913), pp. 45 f. Cf. *Estetica come scienza dell' espressione,* 3d ed. (Bari: G. Laterza & Figli, 1908), pp. 129 ff.

As I see it, such a view does not do justice to the artistic process; for it would break the work of art into two halves, which would then stand in no necessary relation to each other. In actuality, however, the particular manner in which the work of art is expressed belongs not only to the *technique* of the construction of the work but also to its very *conception*. Beethoven's intuition is musical, Phidias' intuition is plastic, Milton's intuition is epic, Goethe's intuition is lyric. In each case this fact involves not only the surface but the very heart of their creative work. It is only with this reflection that we strike the bedrock, the true meaning and profound justification, for the classification of the arts into various "species."

It is easy to discern the *motive* behind Croce's bitter attack upon the doctrine of art genres. By launching this attack he is determined to put a stop to an error which runs through the entire history of aesthetics and which often has caused it to busy itself with problems which lead nowhere. Time and again the attempt has been made to use the determinants of the various art genres and divisions as a basis for establishing a "canon" of the beautiful. On the basis of it, men have sought to arrive at fixed and universal norms for evaluating works of art, with all the consequent disputes as to the superiority of this or that art. In Leonardo da Vinci's *Treatise on Painting* one can discern the zeal with which the battle between painting and poetry was still being waged in the Renaissance. Surely this goal is a mistaken one. It is useless to give a definition of ode, idyl, and tragedy and then to ask if one such work has attained the aim of poetry more perfectly than another. Still more questionable is the attempt to order the various arts in an ascending series and then to ask which can take the place of others in this hierarchy. "A small poem," declares Croce, "stands aesthetically on a par with an epic or with a sketch of an altarpiece, or a fresco; a letter is no less a work of art than a novel." This could very well be the case: but does it follow from this that in its aesthetic meaning and content, a lyric "is" an epic, that a letter "is" a novel?

Croce is able to draw this conclusion simply because, in the construction of his aesthetic he has maintained that the factor of "expression" is the true and the only starting point. He lays almost exclusive emphasis on the supposed fact that art must be expression of private feeling and of private states of emotion; to him, the manner in which they are captured, the direction pursued by the presentation, is immaterial. Not only does this favor the "subjective" aspect; in contrast, the "objective" side of the process becomes little more than an indifferent factor within the "subjective" [synthesis of intuition]. Every manner of artistic intuition becomes "lyrical intuition"—regardless of whether it is realized in [the written] drama, in an epic, in sculpture, in architecture, or on the stage.

> Here the individuality of the intuition refers to the individuality of the expression; here one painting is as different from another as it is from a poem; and painting and poetry have value, not because of the sounds filling the air or the color refractions in the light, but because of what they are able . . . to convey to the mind; hence there is no purpose to be gained in having recourse to abstract means of expression for the construction of a series of species or classes.[8]

It is evident that Croce rejects the doctrine of art genre not only to the extent that it institutes conceptual norms—

8. Croce, *Grundiss der Aesthetik,* p. 36.

this is fully justified—but also inasmuch as it seeks to determine specific concepts of style. Consequently, for Croce, all
differences regarding the *form* of presentation disappear,
or are reduced in significance to mere "physical" differences
in means of presentation. But this very setting-off of "physical" factors from "psychical" factors is thrown into doubt
by the fact of their unconscious "absence" in a great work
of art. Here both factors are so completely merged into each
other that, although they can be distinguished in reflection,
for aesthetic intuition and aesthetic feeling they constitute
an inseparable whole.

Can one really oppose the concrete "intuition" to the
"abstract" means of expression the way Croce attempts to do
and thus treat all differences in the latter sphere as purely
conceptual differences? In the work of art does not the one
imply the other? In purely phenomenological terms, is it
possible to "demonstrate" any kind of uniform primal
layer of aesthetic intuition which continues to remain the
same and which decides upon its mode of execution—
whether in words, sounds, or colors—only at the moment
when it becomes a work of art? Even Croce does not accept
this. He emphatically states that "If one takes the meter,
rhythm, or words from a poem, it is not true, as many suppose, that there still remains the poetic thought: nothing
remains. The poem is born with these words, rhythms, and
meters."[9] But from this it also follows that the aesthetic intuition is born at the same time—i.e., as musical, plastic,
lyric, or dramatic—and that these distinctions are, therefore, not mere verbal notations or labels which we fix on
works of art, and finally, that true differences of style, divergent directions of artistic intention, correspond to these
differences.

9. *Ibid.*

If we take this as established, it is evident that our general problem is encountered in every type of artistic composition and that, on the other hand, it may assume a specific form in each of them. The factor of constancy of form and the factor of "modifiability" of form are encountered in all fields. Clearly, the balance between them does not appear to come about in the same manner. At one time duration and sameness of form seem to have the upper hand; at another time it is change and movement. One can, in a sense, oppose the specificity, fixity, and closedness of the architectonic form to the movement, variability, and variation of the lyrical or musical form. But these are merely differences in emphasis; for even in architecture we discern a dynamic and a rhythmic form, just as in music there is a rigorous statics of form.

Indeed, the lyric appears to be, of all the arts, the most fluid and fleeting. It knows no other being than that which reveals itself in sheer becoming—this becoming is not the objective alteration of things, but the inner motion of the ego itself. If there is an attempt here to hold fast to anything, it is to change as such—the coming and going, the emerging and the vanishing, the suggestion and tantalization of the subtlest stirrings of the soul, and the most transient of its sentiments. If ever the artist has no *ready* world of "forms" to make use of, surely it is here, where for each new moment he must create a new form. And yet, the history of the lyric demonstrates that "duration" is not completely absent from it, that "heterogeneity" is not the only, nor an all-powerful, factor. Even in the lyric, everything which it produces afresh is, nevertheless, always a recollection and an echo.

For there are, after all, only a few great and fundamental themes to which lyric poetry may apply itself. They remain both inexhaustible and unchanging; they are common to all peoples and can hardly be said to have undergone any

change throughout the history of man. Indeed, in no field of
artistic activity is the choice of subject matter so circumscribed as here. The epic poet is always able to construct
new events and the dramatic poet new characters and conflicts. But lyric poetry never leaves the sphere of human
feelings, with the result that it is forever leading one back
to that point where everything else converges. For it, there
is, after all, nothing external; it is always within. This in-
nerness appears infinite, insofar as it is never completely
expressible nor exhaustible; but this is an infinity of content, not of extension. The number of truly lyrical *motifs*
hardly appears to be capable of increase with the passage of
time, nor is this lack of motifs a sign of poverty. Always
lyric poetry resolves itself into the "natural forms of humanity"; yet, it is precisely within the personal, the particular,
the unrepeatable, that it senses the eternal return of the
same. A limited sphere of objects is all it needs in order to
produce a limitless wealth of mood and poetic form. Time
and again we encounter the same objects and the same typical human situations. Love and wine, the rose and the night-
ingale, the pang of separation and the joy of reunion, the
coming into being and the passing away of natural things—
in every age lyric poetry is forever returning to all of these.

The weight of tradition and convention is also to be
found in the history of lyric poetry—indeed, it is felt here
with particular force. But all this weight of tradition is removed or overturned whenever in the course of centuries a
new and really great lyric poet makes his appearance. But
even such a poet can hardly be said to widen the sphere of
lyric "objects" and lyric motifs. Goethe did not hesitate to
link himself to the lyrics of all peoples and all times, both in
his choice of motif and in his choice of form. The *Roman
Elegies* and the *Westöstliche Divan* show how important

such appeals to, and echoes of himself were to him. Still, the one is no more the language of Catullus or Propertius than the other is that of Hafis. What we hear is simply the language of Goethe—the language of moments in a life which are unrepeatable and unique and which he has captured in his poetry.

So it is that in each of the various domains of culture we always encounter this process, which, in its basic structure, is one and the same. Opposition and clash between these two forces—the one seeking preservation and the other seeking renewal—is endless. Any equilibrium which, for a time, may appear to have been attained is never more than an unstable balance of forces, a balance that can break out into a new movement at any point. So it is that, with the growth and development of culture, the pendulum widens its swing—the amplitude of the swing itself continues to increase. As a result, the inner tensions and oppositions also continue to increase in intensity. Still, at no time does this drama of culture become a complete "tragedy of culture." For just as it contains an ultimate defeat so it also contains an ultimate victory. Instead of mutually destroying each other, these two forces nourish one another. The creative movement of the spirit appears to nurture its own antagonist in those very works which it itself has brought forth. For everything created must by its very nature struggle for position against what is emerging and will emerge. But if this movement of the human spirit continually breaks apart *within* its creations, it does not break itself *upon* them. Instead, in the latter it only finds itself forced and stimulated toward new effort, in which it discovers new and unknown powers.

Nowhere does this occur in such suggestive and characteristic form as in the process of change within *religious* thought. Here, in all likelihood, we see the struggle in its profoundest and most convulsive aspect. In it, not only the thought and fantasy but the feeling and will of the whole man are involved. For this time it is no longer a question of finite and particular goals; it is a question of life or death, of being or not being. It is no longer a qualified decision; it concerns the *one* absolute decision. Religion is convinced that to it belongs such an absolute decision. In it man believes himself to have found the eternal, that which endures and upon which the storm of time has no claim. But the promise of this highest good and highest worth at once imposes a specific demand upon the individual; he must accept what it offers; he must renounce his own inner turmoil, his own restless longing. If religion, like all spiritual values [*Güter*], takes its rise from the stream of life, it is nonetheless also true that it is determined, at one and the same time, to break loose from life and overpower it. Here life opens upon the vision of a "transcendent" sphere, which untouched by it, is valid in and of itself, and which remains ever true unto itself. For the sake of this object it must have the strongest internal and external bonds.

Always, the further we go back into the history of religion the firmer these bonds become. The god whose help is being implored will appear only if no word in the prayer formula is altered; the rite loses all religious potency if it is not executed in one and the same unalterable chain of individual acts. In the religion of "primitives" this rigidity of religious formalism encrusts the whole of life. Every least act is met and threatened by religious commands. A welter of tabu prescriptions runs like an iron band around the whole of man's life and presence. But developments within religion show him other and higher bounds. The bond does not cease to exist. And it does not move outward but inward.

The prayer changes from the magical force of words to the invocation of divinity; the offering and the cult act become reconciliation with God. And with this there comes a growth and strengthening of the subjective and the personal [*Individuellen*]. Religion is and remains a body of fixed statements of belief and fixed practical injunctions. These statements are held to be true and the commands valid because they have been revealed and announced by God. But their proclamation is realized nowhere except in souls of the individuals, in the souls of the great founders and prophets of religion.

But here, once again, that basic opposition breaks loose with full force, and here it is felt in its full depth. The I develops beyond all its empirical limits; it acknowledges no barrier between self and divinity; it feels itself to be directly inspired and permeated by God. And by virtue of this immediacy it rejects everything having the character of objective decree, and all that belongs merely to religious tradition. The prophet is determined to build "a new heaven and a new earth."

But here, it must be admitted, in his own being and in his own work, the prophet falls prey to that very force from which he seeks to set men free. He can only throw out fixed and prevailing dogmas by replacing them with his own deeper conviction of divinity. And, in order to give voice to this conviction, he must himself become the one who once again is the creator of religious symbols. So long as he is still inspired and filled with the inner force of the vision, these can only be sensuous images for him. But for those to whom the revelation is imparted the sensuous symbols will once again become dogmas. The accomplishments of every great religious founder show us how he is always stubbornly drawn into this sphere. What for him was living is transformed, and stiffens into dogma. And so it is that here, too, we find the same oscillation which sets in within all forms of culture as they begin to take shape. Even though religion proclaims The Unchanging, The Eternal, and The Absolute, it, too, is unable to elude this process; for, at that moment when [through its prophets] it seeks to become involved in life and to mold it, it is immediately involved in the to and fro, the ceaseless and irresistible rhythm of life itself.

On the basis of these observations we can now define more sharply the specific difference which exists between process [*Werden*] in "nature" and process in "culture." Even nature recognizes no absolute fixity; even organisms, for all the specificity of their form, possess a real freedom. Capacity for change is a fundamental characteristic of all organic things. The "building and rebuilding of organic patterns" is the great theme of all morphology of nature. But the relation between motion and rest, between form and change of form, which prevails in organic nature differs in two respects from the corresponding relation in the creations of culture. Mobility and permanence are the rightful claim of both; but these two factors appear in a different light the moment we shift our gaze from the world of nature to the human world. If we believe ourselves able to demonstrate an ascendency in nature from "lower" to "higher" forms, this is, in fact, a case of transition from one species to the next. Here the genetic viewpoint is always a generic viewpoint. Of necessity, the individual is of no distinctive importance here; in this transition we know nothing concerning the individual, nor have we any need of such knowledge. For the changes which the individual undergoes do not affect the immediate species nor are they an alteration in its life-form. This is the barrier which, as biological fact, is referred to as the non-transmissibility of acquired characteristics. Those non-special variations which do take place in specimens within the plant and animal worlds remain biologically ineffectual; they emerge only to vanish. If we wish to express this evident fact in the language of Weismannian inheritance theory—and we admit, of course, that the question as to the empirical correctness and provability of this theory is yet to be answered— we can say that these biological changes affect only the body, not the "germ plasm" and that, accordingly, they remain on the surface without affecting that deeper layer which determines the development of the species.

But in cultural phenomena this biological barrier has been overcome. In his "symbolic forms"—and they constitute what is non-genetic in his being and gifts—man has found, as it were, the solution to a task which his organic nature was incapable of solving. "Spirit" has accomplished what was denied to "life." Here the coming-to-be and the activity of individuals are linked to that of the species in a very different and profoundly formative manner. What the individual feels, wills, and thinks does not remain enclosed within himself; it is objectified in his work. These works of language, poetry, plastic art, and religion, become the "monuments," the symbols, of recognition and remembrance of human kind. They are "more lasting than bronze"; for within them there remains not only something material; in addition, they are the manifestation of a spirit—manifestation which can be freed from its material covering and awakened to new power whenever a sympathetic and sensitive soul encounters it.

To be sure, there are also countless things in the domain of cultural values which come to nought, which are forever lost to mankind. For these values have a material aspect and this is certainly perishable. The burning of the library at Alexandria annihilated many things of priceless value for our knowledge of antiquity; most of Leonardo's paintings are lost to us because the colors in which they were painted have not lasted. But even in *these* cases the works as such remain tied to the whole of culture as if by invisible threads. If such a work no longer exists in its individual form, still it has produced effects which have made themselves felt in one way or another in the development of culture and have probably determined this process decisively at one point or another.

This does not have reference merely to the great and the rare. The same sort of phenomenon is to be found in the narrowest and smallest spheres of culture. It has been rightly pointed out that in all probability there is no single act of speech which has not influenced "the" language in some manner. The most far-reaching changes in linguistic usages, resulting in phonetic shifts or changes of structure, can result from just such countless acts. It is of decisive significance that in his speech, his art, and all the rest of his forms of culture, man has created, so to speak, a new body which all men share in common. It is perfectly true that the individual human being cannot, as such, transmit to others his own proficiencies, proficiencies which he has acquired through the course of his life. They adhere to the physical "soma" and are not transmitted. Nevertheless, that part of himself which he puts into his work, what is expressed linguistically, in imagery, in plastic form, is *embodied* in language and art and endures henceforth through it. It is this process which distinguishes the mere *transformation* [*Umbildung*] taking place in the sphere of organic emergence from the *formation* [*Bildung*] of humanity. The former is a passive occurrence, the latter is active. Accordingly, the former leads simply to variations, whereas the latter leads to enduring creations. In the last analysis, work is nothing but a human act which by existing solidifies itself, but which claims its origin in this act of embodiment. The creative will and power by which it comes into being continues alive and effective within it and, in turn, calls forth ever new creations.

DATE DUE	BORROWER'S NAME